KV-374-775

WORLD HISTORY IN THE LIGHT OF
ANTHROPOSOPHY

and as a foundation for
knowledge of the human spirit

WORLD HISTORY

IN THE LIGHT OF

ANTHROPOSOPHY

and as a foundation for
knowledge of the human spirit

RUDOLF STEINER

Nine lectures given in Dornach
24 December 1923 to 1 January 1924
during the Foundation Meeting
of the General Anthroposophical Society

Lectures I to VIII translated by George and Mary Adams
Lecture IX translated by Dorothy Osmond

RUDOLF STEINER PRESS
LONDON

First published in English by Anthroposophical Publishing
Company, London, 1950
Second Edition (enlarged), Rudolf Steiner Press, 1977

Translated from shorthand reports unrevised by the lecturer. The
German text is published in: *Die Weltgeschichte in anthropo-
sophischer Beleuchtung und als Grundlage der Erkenntnis des
Menschengeistes* (Vol. No. 233 in the *Bibliographical Survey*, 1961)

This English edition is published in agreement with the *Rudolf
Steiner-Nachlassverwaltung*, Dornach, Switzerland

© Rudolf Steiner Press, London, 1977

ISBN 085440 315 9 (cased)
316 7 (paper)

Made and printed in Great Britain by
The Camelot Press Ltd, Southampton

CONTENTS

I

IN THE EVENING HOURS of our Christmas Gathering, I should like to give you a kind of survey of human evolution on the earth, that may help us to become more intimately conscious of the nature and being of present-day man. For at this time in man's history, when we can see already in preparation events of extraordinary importance for the whole civilisation of humanity, every thinking man must be inclined to ask : ' How has the present configuration, the present make-up of the human soul arisen ? How has it come about through the long course of evolution ? ' For it cannot be denied that the present only becomes comprehensible as we try to understand its origin in the past.

The present age is however one that is peculiarly prejudiced in its thought about the evolution of man and of mankind. It is commonly believed that, as regards his life of soul and spirit, man has always been essentially the same as he is to-day throughout the whole of the time that we call history. True, in respect of knowledge, it is imagined that in ancient times human beings were childlike, that they believed in all kinds of fancies, and that man has only really become clever in the scientific sense in modern times ; but if we look away from the actual sphere of knowledge, it is generally held that the soul-constitution which man has to-day was also possessed by the ancient Greek and by the ancient Oriental. Even though it be admitted that modifications may have occurred in detail, yet on the whole it is supposed that throughout the historical period everything in the life of the soul has been as it is to-day. Then we go on to assume a prehistoric life of man, and say that nothing is really known of this. Going still further back, we picture man in a kind of animal form. Thus, in the first place, as we trace back in

7

historical time, we see a soul-life undergoing comparatively little change. Then the picture disappears in a kind of cloud, and before that again we see man in his animal imperfection as a kind of higher ape-being. Such is approximately the usual conception of to-day.

Now all this rests on an extraordinary prejudice, for in forming such a conception, we do not take the trouble to observe the important differences that exist in the soul-constitution of a man of the present-time, as compared even with that of a relatively not very far distant past,—say, of the 11th, 10th, or 9th century A.D. The difference goes deeper when we compare the constitution of soul in the human being of to-day and in a contemporary of the Mystery of Golgotha, or in a Greek ; while if we go over to the ancient Oriental world of which the Greek civilisation was, in a sense, a kind of colony, we find there a disposition of soul utterly different from that of the man of to-day. I should like to show you from real instances how man lived in the East, let us say, ten thousand, or fifteen thousand years ago, and how different he was in nature from the Greek, and how still more different from what we ourselves are.

Let us first call to mind our own soul-life. I will take an example from it. We have a certain experience ; and of this experience, in which we take part through our senses, or through our personality in some other way, we form an idea, a concept, and we retain this idea in our thought. After a certain time the idea may arise again out of our thought into our conscious soul-life, as memory. You have perhaps to-day a memory-experience that leads you back to experiences in perception of some ten years ago. Now try and understand exactly what that really means. Ten years ago you experienced something. Ten years ago you may have visited a gathering of men and women. You formed an idea of each one of these persons, of their appearance and so on. You experienced what they said to you, and what you did in common with them. All that, in the form of pictures, may arise before you to-day. It is an inner soul-picture that is present within you, connected with the event which occurred ten years ago. Now not only according to Science, but according to a general feeling,—which is, of course, experienced by man to-day in an extremely weak form, but which nevertheless *is* experienced,—according to this general feeling man localises such a memory-concept which brings back a past experience, in his head. He says :— ' What lives as the memory of an experience is present in my head.'

Now let us jump a long way back in human evolution, and consider the early population of the Orient, of which the Chinese and Indians as we know them in history were only the late descendants : that is, let us go back really thousands of years. Then, if we contemplate a human being of that ancient epoch, we find that he did not live in such a way as to say : ' I have in my head the memory of something I have experienced, something I have undergone, in external life.' He had no such inner feeling or experience ; it simply did not exist for him. His head was not filled with thoughts and ideas. The present-day man thinks in his superficial way that as we to-day have ideas, thoughts, and concepts, so human beings always possessed these, as far back as history records ; but that is not the case. If with spiritual insight we go back far enough, we meet with human beings who did not have ideas, concepts, thoughts at all in their head, who did not experience any such abstract content of the head, but, strange as it may seem, experienced the whole head ; they perceived and felt their whole head. These men did not give themselves up to abstractions as we do. To experience ideas in the head was something quite foreign to them, but they knew how to experience their own head. And as you, when you have a memory-picture, refer the memory-picture to an experience, as a relationship exists between your memory-picture and the experience, similarly these men related the experience of their head to the Earth, to the whole Earth. They said :—' There exists in the Cosmos the Earth. And there exists in the Cosmos I myself, and as a part of me, my head ; and the head which I carry on my shoulders is the cosmic memory of the Earth. The Earth existed earlier ;

my head later. That I have a head is due to the memory, the cosmic memory of earthly existence. The earthly existence is always there. But the whole configuration, the whole shape of the human head, is in relation to the whole Earth.' Thus an ancient Eastern felt in his own head the being of the Earth-planet itself. He said : ' Out of the whole great cosmic existence the Gods have created, have generated the Earth with its kingdoms of Nature, the Earth

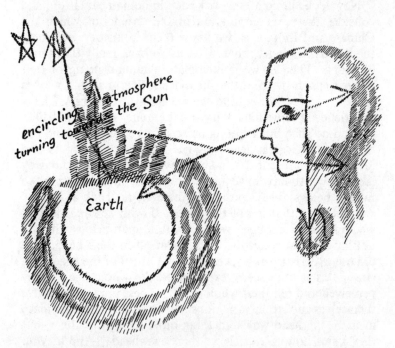

with its rivers and mountains. I carry on my shoulders my head ; and this head of mine is a true picture of the Earth. This head, with the blood flowing in it, is a true picture of the Earth with the land and water coursing over it. The configuration of mountains on the Earth repeats itself in my head in the configurations of my brain ; I carry on my shoulders my own image of the Earth-planet.' Exactly as our modern man refers his memory-picture to his experience, so did the man of old refer his entire head to the Earth-planet. A considerable difference in inner perception!

Further, when we consider the periphery of the Earth, and fit it, as it were, into our vision of things, we feel this air surrounding the Earth as air permeated by the Sun's warmth and light ; and in a certain sense, we can say : ' The Sun lives in the atmosphere of the Earth.' The Earth opens herself to the Cosmic universe ; the activities that come forth from herself she yields up to the encircling atmosphere, and opens herself to receive the activities of the Sun. Now each human being, in those ancient times, experienced the region of the Earth on which he lived as of peculiar importance. An ancient Eastern would feel some portion of the surface of the Earth as his own ; beneath him the earth, and above him the encircling atmosphere turned towards the Sun. The rest of the Earth that lay to left and right, in front and behind—all the rest of the Earth merged into a general whole.

Thus if an ancient Oriental lived, for example, on Indian soil, he experienced the Indian soil as especially important for him ; but everything else on the Earth, East, West, South of him, disappeared into the whole. He did not concern himself much with the way in which the Earth in these other parts was bounded by the rest of Cosmic space ; while on the other hand not only was the soil on which he lived something important, but the extension of the Earth into Cosmic space in this region became a matter of great moment to him. The way in which he was able to breathe on this particular soil was felt by him as an inner experience of special importance.

To-day we are not in the habit of asking, how does one breathe in this or that place ? We are of course still subject to favourable or unfavourable conditions for breathing, but we are no longer so conscious of the fact. For an ancient Oriental this was different. The way in which he was able to breathe was for him a very deep experience, and so were many other things too that depend on the character

11

of the Earth's relation and contact with cosmic space. All that goes to make up the Earth, the whole Earth, was felt by the human being of those early times as that which lived in his head.

Now the head is enclosed by the hard firm bones of the skull, it is shut in above, on two sides and behind. But it has certain exits ; it has a free opening downwards towards the chest. And it was of special importance for the man of olden time to feel how the head opens with relative freedom in the direction of the chest. (*See Drawing*). And as he had to feel the inner configuration of the head as an image of the Earth, so he had to bring the environment of the Earth, all that is above and around the Earth, into connection with the opening downwards, the turning towards the heart. In this he saw an image of how the Earth opens to the Cosmos. It was a mighty experience for a man of those ancient times when he said : ' In my head I feel the whole Earth. But this Earth opens to my chest which carries within it my heart. And that which takes place between head, chest and heart is an image of what is borne out from my life into the Cosmos, borne out to the surrounding atmosphere that is open to the Sun.'

A great experience it was for him, and one of deep meaning, when he was able to say : ' Here in my head lives the Earth. When I go deeper, there the Earth is turning towards the Sun; my heart is the image of the Sun.' In this way did the man of olden times attain what corresponds to our life of feeling.

We have the abstract life of feeling still. But who of us knows anything directly of his heart ? Through anatomy and physiology, we think we know something, but it is about as much as we know of some papier-maché model of the heart that we may have before us. On the other hand, what we have as a feeling-experience of the world, that the man of olden times did not have. In place of it he had the experience of his heart. Just as we relate our feeling to the world in which we live, just as we feel whether we love a man or meet him with antipathy, whether we like this or that flower, whether we incline towards this or that, just as we relate our feelings to the world—but to a world torn out, as it were, in airy abstraction, from the solid, firm Cosmos—in the same way did the ancient Oriental relate his heart to the Cosmos, that is, to that which goes away from the Earth in the direction of the Sun.

Again, we say to-day : I will walk. We know that our will lives in our limbs. The ancient man of the East had an essentially different experience. What we call ' will ' was quite unknown to him. We judge quite wrongly when we believe that what we call thinking, feeling and willing were present among the ancient Eastern races. It was not at all the case. They had head experiences, which were Earth experiences. They had chest or heart experiences, which were experiences of the environment of the Earth as far out as the Sun. The Sun corresponds to the heart experience. Then they had a further experience, a feeling of expanding and stretching out into their limbs. They became conscious and aware of their own humanity in the movement of their legs and feet, or of their arms and hands. They themselves were within the movements. And in this expansion of the inner being into the limbs, they felt a direct picture of their connection with the starry worlds. (*See Drawing*). ' In my head I have a picture of the Earth. Where my head opens freely downwards into the chest and reaches down to my heart,I have a picture of what lives in the Earth's environment. In what I experience as the forces of my arms and hands, of my feet and legs, I have something which represents the relation the Earth bears to the stars that live far out there in cosmic space.'

When therefore man wanted to express the experience he had as ' willing ' human being—to use the language of to-day, —he did not say : I walk. We can see that from the very words that he used. Nor did he say : I sit down. If we investigate the ancient languages in respect of their finer content, we find everywhere that for the action which we describe by saying : I walk, the ancient Oriental would have said : Mars impels me, Mars is active in me. Going forward was felt as a Mars impulse in the legs.

Grasping hold of something, feeling and touching with the hands, was expressed by saying : Venus works in me. Pointing out something to another person was expressed by saying : Mercury works in me. Even when a rude person called some one's attention by giving him a push or a kick, the action would be described by saying : Mercury was working in that person. Sitting down was a Jupiter activity, and lying down, whether for rest or from sheer laziness, was expressed by saying : I give myself over to the impulses of Saturn. Thus man felt in his limbs the wide spaces of the Cosmos out beyond. He knew that when he went away from the Earth out into cosmic space, he came into the Earth's environment and then into the starry spheres. If he went downwards from his head, he passed through the very same experience, only this time within his own being. In his head he was in the Earth, in his chest and heart he was in the environment of the Earth, in his limbs he was in the starry Cosmos beyond.

From a certain point of view such an experience is perfectly possible for man. Alas for us, poor men of to-day, who can experience only abstract thoughts ! What are these in reality, for the most part ? We are very proud of them, but we quite forget what is far beyond the cleverest of them,—our head ; our head is much more rich in content than the very cleverest of our abstract thoughts. Anatomy and physiology know little of the marvel and mystery of the convolutions of the brain, but one single convolution of the brain is more majestic and more powerful than the abstract knowledge of the greatest genius. There was once a time on the Earth when man was not merely conscious as we are of thoughts lying around, so to speak, but was conscious of his own head ; he felt the head as the image of the Earth, and he felt this or that part of the head—let us say, the optic thalamus or the corpora quadrigemina—as the image of a certain, physical mountainous configuration of the Earth. He did not then merely relate his heart to the Sun in accordance with some abstract theory, he felt : ' My head stands in the same relation to my chest, to my heart, as the Earth does to the

14

Sun.' That was the time when man had grown together, in his whole life, with the Cosmic Universe ; he had become one with the Cosmos. And this found expression in his whole life.

Through the fact that we to-day put our puny thinking in the place of our head, through this very fact we are able to have a conceptual memory, we are able to remember things in thought. We form pictures in thought of what we have experienced as abstract memories in our head. That could not be done by a man of olden times who did not have thoughts, but still had his head. He could not form memory pictures. And so, in those regions of the Ancient East where people were still conscious of their head, but had as yet no thoughts and hence no memories, we find developed to a remarkable degree something of which people are again beginning to feel the need to-day. For a long time such a thing has not been necessary, and if to-day the need for it is returning it is due to what I can only call slovenliness of soul.

If in that time of which I have spoken one were to enter the region inhabited by people who were still conscious of their head, chest, heart and limbs, one would see on every hand small pegs placed in the earth and marked with some sign. Or here and there a sign made upon a wall. Such memorials were to be found scattered over all inhabited regions. Wherever anything happened, a man would set up some kind of memorial, and when he came back to the place, he lived through the event over again in the memorial he had made. Man had grown together with the earth, he had become one with it with his head. To-day he merely makes a note of some event in his head. As I have pointed out already, we are beginning once more to find it necessary to make notes not only in our head but also in a note-book ; this is due as I said, to slovenliness of soul, but we shall nevertheless require to do it more and more. At that time however there was no such thing as making notes even in one's head, because thoughts and ideas were simply non-existent. Instead, the land was dotted over with signs.

And from this habit, so naturally acquired by men in olden times, has arisen the whole custom of making monuments and memorials.

Everything that has happened in the historical evolution of mankind has its origin and cause in the inner being of man. If we were but honest, we should have to admit that we modern men have not the faintest knowledge of the deeper basis of this custom of erecting memorials. We set them up from habit. They are however the relics of the ancient monuments and signs put up by man in a time when he had no memory such as we have to-day but was taught, in any place where he had some experience, there to set up a memorial, so that when he came that way again he might re-experience the event in his head; for the head can call up again everything that has connection with the earth. ' We give over to the earth what our head has experienced '—was a principle of olden times.

And so we have to point to a very early time in the ancient East, the epoch of *localised memory*, when everything of the nature of memory was connected with the setting up of signs and memorials on the earth. Memory was not within, but without. Everywhere were memorial tablets and memorial stones. It was localised memory, a remembering connected with place.

Even to-day it is still of no small value for a man's spiritual evolution that he should sometimes make use of his capacity for this kind of memory, for a memory that is not within him but is unfolded in connection with the outer world. It is good sometimes to say : I will not *remember* this or that, but I will set here or there a *sign*, or token ; or, I will let my soul unfold an experience about certain things, only in connection with signs or tokens. I will, for instance, hang a picture of the Madonna in a corner of my room, and when the picture is before me, I will experience in my soul all that I can experience by turning with my whole soul to the Madonna. For there is a subtle relation to a thing belonging so intimately to the home as does the picture of the Madonna that we meet with in the homes of the people, when

16

we go a little way eastwards in Europe; we have not even to go as far as Russia, we find them everywhere in Central Europe. All experience of this nature is in reality a relic of the epoch of localised memory. The memory is outside, it attaches to the place.

A second stage is reached when man passes from localised to *rhythmic memory*. Thus we have first, localised memory; and secondly, rhythmic memory.

We have now come to the time when, not from any conscious, subtle finesse, but right out of his own inner being, man had developed the need of living in rhythm. He felt a need so to reproduce, within himself, what he heard that a rhythm was formed. If his experience of a cow, for instance, suggested 'moo,' he did not simply call her 'moo,' but 'moo-moo,'—perhaps, in very ancient times, 'moo-moo-moo." That is to say, the perception was as it were piled up in repetition, so as to produce rhythm. You can follow the same process in the formation of many words to-day; and you can observe how little children still feel the need of these repetitions. We have here again a heritage come down from the time when rhythmic memory prevailed, the time when man had no memory at all of what he had merely experienced, but only of what he experienced in rhythmic form,—in repetitions, in rhythmic repetition. There had to be at any rate some similarity between a sequence of words. 'Might and main,' 'stock and stone'—such setting of experience in rhythmic sequence is a last relic of an extreme longing to bring everything into rhythm; for in this second epoch, that followed the epoch of localised memory, what was not set into rhythm was not retained. It is from this rhythmic memory that the whole ancient art of verse developed—indeed all metrical poetry.

Only in the third stage does that develop which we still know to-day,—*temporal memory*, when we no longer have a point in space to which memory attaches, nor are any longer dependent on rhythm, but when that which is inserted into the course of time can be evoked again

17

later. This quite abstract memory of ours is the third stage in the evolution of memory.

Let us now call to mind the point of time in human evolution when rhythmic memory passes over into temporal memory, when that memory first made its appearance which we with our lamentable abstractness of thought take entirely as a matter of course ; the memory whereby we evoke some-thing in picture-form, no longer needing to make use of semi-conscious or unconscious rhythmic repetitions in order to call it up again.

The epoch of the transition from rhythmic memory to temporal memory is the time when the ancient East was sending colonies to Greece,—the beginning of the colonies planted from Asia in Europe. When the Greeks relate stories of the heroes who came over from Asia and Egypt to settle on Grecian soil, they are in reality relating how the great heroes went forth from the land of rhythmic memory to seek a climate where rhythmic memory could pass over into temporal memory, into a remembering in time.

We are thus able to define quite exactly the time in history when this transition took place,—namely, the time of the rise of Greece. For that which may be called the Mother-land of Greece was the home of a people with strongly developed rhythmic memory. There rhythm lived. The ancient East is indeed only rightly understood when we see it as the land of rhythm. And if we place Paradise only so far back as the Bible places it, if we lay the scene of Paradise in Asia, then we have to see it as a land where purest rhythms resounded through the Cosmos and awoke again in man as rhythmic memory,—a land where man lived not only as experiencing rhythm in a Cosmos, but as himself a creator of rhythm.

Listen to the Bhagavad-Gita and you will catch the after-echo of that mighty rhythm that once lived in the experience of man. You will hear its echo also in the Vedas, and you will even hear it in the poetry and literature—to use a modern word—of Western Asia. In all these live the echoes of that rhythm which once filled the whole of Asia with

18

majestic content and, bearing within it the mysteries of the environment of the Earth, made these resound again in the human breast, in the beat of the human heart. Then we come to a still more ancient time, when rhythmic memory leads back into localised memory, when man did not even have rhythmic memories but was taught, in the place where he had had an experience, there to erect a memorial. When he was away from the place, he needed no memorial; but when he came thither again he had to recall the experience. Yet it was not he who recalled it to himself; the memorial, the very Earth, recalled it to him. As the head is the image of the Earth, so for the man of localised memory the memorial in the Earth evoked its own image in the head. Man lived completely with the Earth; in his connection with the Earth he had his memory.

The Gospels contain a passage that recalls this kind of memory, where we are told that Christ wrote something in the Earth.

The period we have thus defined as the transition from localised memory to rhythmic memory is the time when ancient Atlantis was declining and the first Post-Atlantean peoples were wandering eastward in the direction of Asia. For we have first the wanderings from ancient Atlantis— the continent that to-day forms the bed of the Atlantic Ocean—right across Europe into Asia, and later the wanderings back again from Asia into Europe. The migration of the Atlantean peoples to Asia marks the transition from localised memory to rhythmic memory, which latter finds its completion in the spiritual life of Asia. The colonisation of Greece marks the transition from rhythmic memory to temporal memory—the memory that we still carry within us to-day.

1. Localised Memory.
2. Rhythmic Memory.
3. Temporal Memory.

And within this evolution of memory lies the whole development of civilisation between the Atlantean catastrophe and the rise of Greece,—all that resounds to us from ancient

Asia, coming to us in the form of legend and saga rather than as history. We shall arrive at no understanding of the evolution of humanity on the Earth by looking principally to the external phenomena, by investigating the external documents ; rather do we need to fix our attention on the evolution of what is within man ; we must consider how such a thing as the faculty of memory has developed, passing in its development from without into the inner being of man.

You know how much the power of memory means for the man of to-day. You will have heard of persons who through some condition of illness suddenly find that a portion of their past life, which they ought to remember quite easily, has been completely wiped out. A terrible experience of this kind befell a friend of mine before his death. One day he left his home, bought a ticket at the railway station for a certain place, alighted there and bought another ticket. He did all this, having lost for the time the memory of his life up to the moment of buying the ticket. He carried everything out quite sensibly. His reason was sound. But his memory was blotted out. And he found himself, when his memory came back, in a Casual Ward in Berlin. It was afterwards proved that in the interval he had wandered over half Europe, without being able to connect the experience with the earlier experiences of his life. Memory did not re-awaken in him till he had found his way—he himself did not know how—into a Casual Ward in Berlin.

This is only one of countless cases which we meet with in life and which show us how the soul-life of the man of to-day is not intact unless the threads of memory are able to reach back unbroken to a certain period after birth.

With the men of olden time who had developed a localised memory, this was not the case. They knew nothing of these threads of memory. They, on the other hand, would have been unhappy in their soul-life, they would have felt as we feel when something robs us of our self, if they had not been surrounded by memorials which recalled to them what they had experienced ; and not alone by memorials which they themselves had set up, but memorials too erected by their forefathers, or by their brothers and sisters, similar in configuration to their own and bringing them into contact with their own kinsmen. Whereas we are conscious of something inward as the condition for keeping our Self intact, for these men of bygone times the condition was to be sought outside themselves—in the world without.

We have to let the whole picture of this change in man's soul pass before our eyes in order to realise its significance in the history of man's evolution. It is by observing such things as these that light begins to be thrown upon history. To-day I wanted to show, by a special example, how man's mind and soul have evolved in respect of one faculty—the faculty of memory. We shall go on to see in the course of the succeeding lectures how the events of history begin to reveal themselves in their true shape when we can thus illumine them with light derived from knowledge of the human soul.

II

FROM THE FOREGOING LECTURE it will be clear to you that it is only possible to gain a correct view of the historical evolution of humanity when one takes into consideration the totally different conditions of mind and soul that prevailed during the various epochs. In the first part of my lecture I attempted to define the Asiatic period of evolution, the genuine ancient East, and we saw that we have to look back to the time when the descendants of the races of Atlantis were finding their way eastwards after the Atlantean catastrophe, moving from west to east and gradually peopling Europe and Asia. All that took place in ancient Asia in connection with these peoples was under the influence of a condition of soul accustomed and attuned to rhythm. At the beginning of the Asiatic period we have still a distant echo of what was present in all its fullness in Atlantis—the localised memory. During the Oriental evolution this localised memory passed over into rhythmic memory, and I showed how with the Greek evolution that great change came about which brought in a new kind of memory, the temporal memory. This means that the Asiatic period of evolution (we are now speaking of what may rightly be called the Asiatic period, for what history refers to is in reality a later and decadent period) was an age of men altogether differently constituted from the men of later times. And the external events of history were in those days much more dependent than in later times on the character and constitution of man's inner life. What lived in man's mind and soul lived too in his entire being. A separated life of thought and feeling, such as we have to-day was unknown. A thinking that does not feel itself to be connected with the inner processes of the human head, was

23

unknown. So too was the abstract feeling that knows no connection with the circulation of the blood. Man had in those times a thinking that was inwardly experienced as a " happening " in the head, a feeling that was experienced in the rhythm of the breath, in the circulation of the blood, and so on. Man experienced his whole being in undivided unity.

All this was closely connected with the altogether different experience man had of his relation to the world about him, to the Cosmos, to the spiritual and the physical in the Cosmic Whole. The man of the present day lives, let us say, in town or in the country, and his experience varies accordingly. He is surrounded by woods, rivers and mountains ; or, if he lives in town, bricks and mortar meet his gaze on every hand. When he speaks of the cosmic and supersensible, where does he think it is ? He can point to no sphere within which he can conceive of what is cosmic and supersensible as having place. It is nowhere to be laid hold of, he cannot grasp it : even spiritually, he cannot grasp it. But this was not so in that ancient oriental stream of evolution. To an Oriental, the world around him which we to-day call our physical environment, was the lowest portion of a Cosmos conceived as a unity. Man had around him what is contained in the three kingdoms of nature, he had around him the rivers, mountains, and so forth ; but for him this environment was permeated through and through with Spirit, interpenetrated and interwoven with Spirit. The Oriental of ancient time would say : I live with the mountains, I live with the rivers ; but I live also with the elemental beings of the mountains and of the rivers. I live in the physical realm, but this physical realm is the body of a spiritual realm. Around me is the spiritual world, the lowest spiritual world.

There below was this realm that for us has become the earthly realm. Man lived in it. But he pictured to himself that where this realm ends another realm begins, then again above that another ; and finally the highest realm which it is possible to reach. And if we were to name these realms in accordance with the language that has become current with us in anthroposophical knowledge—the ancient Oriental had other names for them, but that does not matter, we will name them as they are for us—then we should have above, for the highest realm, the First Hierarchy : Seraphim, Cherubim, Thrones ; then the Second Hierarchy : Kyriotetes, Dynamis, Exusiai ; and the Third Hierarchy : Archai, Archangels, Angels.

And now comes the fourth realm where human beings live, the realm wherein according to our method of cognition we to-day place the mere objects and processes of Nature, but where the ancient Oriental felt the whole of Nature penetrated with the elemental spirits of water and of earth. This was Asia. Asia meant the lowest spirit realm, in which he, as human being, lived. You must remember that the present-day conception of things that we have in our ordinary consciousness was unknown to the man of those times. It would be nonsense to suppose that it were in any way possible for him to imagine such a thing as matter devoid of spirit. To speak as we do, of oxygen and nitrogen would have been a sheer impossibility for the ancient Oriental. To him oxygen was spirit, it was that spiritual thing which worked as a stimulating and quickening agent on what already possessed life, accelerating the life-processes in a living organism. Nitrogen, which we think of to-day as contained in the atmosphere together with oxygen, was also spiritual ; it was that which weaves throughout the Cosmos, working upon what is living and organic in such a way as to prepare it to receive a soul-nature. Such was the knowledge the Oriental of old had, for example, of oxygen and nitrogen. And he knew all the processes of Nature in this way, in their connection with spirit ; for the present-day conceptions were unknown to him. There were a few individuals who knew them, and they were the Initiates. The rest of mankind had as their ordinary everyday consciousness a consciousness very similar to a waking dream ; it was a dream condition that with us only occurs in abnormal experiences.

The ancient Oriental went about with these dreams. He looked on the mountains, rivers and clouds, and saw everything in the way that things can be seen and heard in this dream condition. Picture to yourself what may happen to the man of to-day in a dream. He is asleep. Suddenly there appears before him a dream-picture of a flaring fire. He hears the call of ' Fire ! ' Outside in the street a fire engine is passing, to put out a fire somewhere or other. But what a difference between the conception of the work of the fire-brigade that can be formed by the human intellect in its matter-of-fact way with the aid of ordinary sense-perception, and the pictures that a dream can conjure up ! For the ancient Oriental, however, all his experiences manifested themselves in such dream-pictures. Everything outside in the kingdoms of Nature was transformed in his soul into pictures.

In these dream-pictures man experienced the elemental spirits of water, earth, air and fire. And sleep brought him again other experiences. Sleep for him was not that deep heavy sleep we have when we lie, as we say, ' like a log ' and know nothing of ourselves. I believe there are people who sleep so in these days, are there not ? But then there was no such thing : even in sleep man had still a dull form of consciousness. While on the one hand he was, as we now say, resting his body, the spiritual was weaving within him in a spiritual activity of the external world. And in this weaving he perceived the Beings of the Third Hierarchy. Asia he perceived in his ordinary waking-dream condition, that is to say in what was the everyday consciousness of that time. At night, in sleep, he perceived the Third Hierarchy. And from time to time there entered into his sleep a still more dim and dark consciousness, but a consciousness that graved its experiences deeply into his thought and feeling. Thus these Eastern peoples had first their everyday consciousness where everything was changed into Imaginations and pictures. The pictures were not so real as those of still older times, for example the time of Atlantis or Lemuria, or of the Moon epoch. Nevertheless they were still there, even during this Asiatic evolution. By day, then, men had these pictures. And in sleep they had an experience which they might have clothed in the following words :—We ' sleep away ' the ordinary earthly existence, we enter the realm of the Angels, Archangels and Archai and live among them. The soul sets itself free from the organism and lives among the Beings of the higher Hierarchies.

Men knew at the same time that whereas they lived in Asia with gnomes, undines, sylphs and salamanders, that is with the elemental spirits of the earth, water, air and fire,— in sleep, while the body rested, they experienced the Beings of the Third Hierarchy in the planetary existence, in all that lives in the whole planetary system belonging to the Earth.

There were however moments when the sleeper would feel : An utterly strange region is approaching me. It is taking me to itself, it is drawing me away from earthly existence. He did not feel this while immersed in the Beings of the Third Hierarchy, but only when a still deeper condition of sleep intervened. Though there was never a real consciousness of what took place during the sleep-condition of the third kind, nevertheless what was then experienced from the Second Hierarchy impressed itself deep into the whole being of man. And the experience remained in man's feeling when he awoke. He could then say : I have been graciously blessed by higher Spirits, whose life is beyond the planetary existence. Thus did these ancient peoples speak of that Hierarchy which embraces the Kyriotetes, the Dynamis and the Exusiai. What we are now describing are the ordinary states of consciousness of this ancient Asiatic period. The first two states of consciousness—the waking-sleeping, sleeping-waking and the sleep, in which the Third Hierarchy were present—were experienced by all men. And many, through a special endowment of Nature, experienced also the intervention of a deeper sleep, during which the Second Hierarchy played into human consciousness.

27

And the Initiates in the Mysteries,—they received a still further degree of consciousness. Of what nature was this ? The answer is astonishing; for the fact is, the Initiate of the ancient East acquired the same consciousness that you have now by day ! You develop it in a perfectly natural way in your second or third year of life. No ancient Oriental ever attained this state of consciousness in a natural way ; he had to develop it artificially in himself. He had to develop it out of the waking-dreaming, dreaming-waking. As long as he went about with this waking-dreaming, dreaming-waking, he saw everywhere pictures, rendering only in more or less symbolic fashion what we see to-day in clear sharp outlines ; as an Initiate however he attained to see things as we see them to-day in our ordinary consciousness. The Initiates, by means of their developed consciousness, attained to learn what every boy and girl learns at school to-day. The difference between their consciousness and the normal consciousness of to-day is not that the content was different. Of course the abstract forms of letters which we have to-day were unknown then ; written characters were in more intimate connection with the things and processes of the Cosmos. Reading and writing were nevertheless learned in those days by the Initiates ; although of course by them alone, for reading and writing can only be learned with that clear intellectual consciousness which is the natural one for the man of to-day.

Supposing that somewhere or other this world of the ancient East were to re-appear, inhabited by human beings having the kind of consciousness they had in those olden times, and you were to come among them with your consciousness of the present day, then for them you would all be initiates. The difference does not lie in the content of consciousness. You would be initiates. But the moment the people recognised you as initiates, they would immediately drive you out of the land by every means in their power ; for it would be quite clear to them that an initiated person ought not to know things in the way we know them to-day. He ought not, for example, to be able to write as we are able to write to-day. If I were to transport myself into the mind of a man of that time, and were to meet such a pseudo-initiate, that is to say, an ordinary clever man of the present day, I should find myself saying of him : He can write, he makes signs on paper that mean something, and he has no idea how devilish it is to do such a thing without carrying in him the consciousness that it may only be done in the service of divine cosmic consciousness ; he does not know that a man may only make such signs on paper when he can feel how God works in his hand, in his very fingers, works in his soul, enabling it to express itself through these letters. Therein lies the whole difference between the initiates of olden time and the ordinary man of the present day. It is not a difference in the content of consciousness, but in the way of comprehending and understanding the thing. Read my book *Christianity as Mystical Fact*, of which a new edition has recently appeared, and you will find right at the beginning the same indication as to the essential nature of the initiate of olden times. It is in point of fact always so in the course of world-evolution. That which develops in man at a later period in a natural way had in former epochs to be won through initiation.

Through such a thing as I have brought to your notice, you will be able to detect the radical difference between the condition of mind and soul prevalent among the Eastern peoples of prehistoric times and that of a later civilisation. It was another mankind that could call Asia the last or lowest heaven and understand by that their own land, the Nature that was round about them. They knew where the lowest heaven was.

Compare this with the conceptions men have to-day. How far is the man of the present time from regarding all he sees around him as the lowest heaven ! Most people cannot think of it as the ' lowest ' heaven for the simple reason that they have no knowledge of any heaven at all !

Thus we see how in that ancient Eastern time the Spiritual entered deeply into Nature, into all natural existence. But now we find also among these peoples something which to most of us in the present day may easily appear extremely barbarous. To a man of that time it would have appeared terribly barbarous if someone had been able to write in the feeling and attitude of mind in which we to-day are able to write ; it would have seemed positively devilish to him. But when we to-day on the other hand see how it was accepted in those times as something quite natural and as a matter of course that a people should remove from West to East, should conquer—often with great cruelty—another people already in occupation and make slaves of them, then such a thing is bound to appear barbarous to very many of us.

This is, however, broadly speaking, the substance of oriental history over the whole of Asia. Whilst men had as I have described, a high spiritual conception of things, their external history ran its course in a series of conquests and enslavements. Undoubtedly that appears to many people as extremely barbarous. To-day, although wars of aggression do still sometimes occur, men have an uneasy conscience about them. And this is true even of those who support and defend such wars ; they are not quite easy in their conscience.

In those times, however, man had a perfectly clear conscience as regards these wars of aggression, he felt that such conquest was willed of the Gods. The longing for peace, the love of peace, that arose later and spread over a large part of Asia, is really the product of a much later civilisation. The acquisition of land by conquest and the enslavement of its population is a salient feature of the early civilisation of Asia. The farther we go back into prehistoric times, the more do we find this kind of conquest going on. The conquests of Xerxes and others of his time were in truth but faint shadows of what went on in earlier ages.

Now there is a quite definite principle underlying these conquests. As a result of the states of consciousness which I have described to you, man stood in an altogether different relation to his fellow man and also to the world around him. Certain differences between different parts of the inhabited Earth have to-day lost their chief meaning. At that time these differences made themselves felt in quite another way. Let me put before you, as an example, something which frequently occurred.

Suppose a conquering people has made its way from the North of Asia, spread itself out over some other region of Asia and made the population subject to it. What has really happened?

In characteristic instances that are a true expression of the trend of historical evolution, we find that the aggressors were—as a people or as a race—young, full of youth-forces. Now what does it mean to-day to be young? What does it mean for men of our present epoch of evolution? It means to bear within one in every moment of life sufficient of the forces of death to provide for those soul-forces that need the dying processes in man. For, as you know, we have within us, the sprouting, germinating forces of life, but these life forces are not the forces that make us reflective, thoughtful beings ; on the contrary, they make us weak, unconscious. The death forces, the forces of destruction, which are also continually active within us—and are overcome again and again during sleep by the life forces, so that not until the end of life do we gather together all the death forces in us in the one final event of death—these forces it is that induce reflection, self-consciousness. This is how it is with present-day humanity. Now a young race, a young people, such as I have described, suffered from its own over-strong life forces, and continually had the feeling : I feel my blood beating perpetually against the walls of my body. I cannot endure it. My consciousness will not become reflective consciousness. Because of my very youthfulness I cannot develop my full humanity.

An ordinary man would not have spoken thus, but the initiates spoke in this way in the Mysteries, and it was the initiates who guided and directed the whole course of history.

Here was then a people who had too much youth, too much life forces, too little in them of that which could bring about reflection and thought. They left their land and

31

conquered a region where an older people lived, a people which had in some way or other taken into itself the forces of death, because it had already become decadent. The younger nation went out against the older and brought it into subjection. It was not necessary that a blood-bond should be established between conquerors and enslaved. That which worked unconsciously in the soul between them worked in a rejuvenating way ; it worked on the reflective faculties. What the conqueror required from the slaves whom he now had in his court was influence upon his consciousness. He had only to turn his attention to these slaves and the longing for unconsciousness was quenched in his soul, reflective consciousness began to dawn.

What we have to attain to-day as individuals was attained at that time by living together with others. A people who faced the world as conquerors and lords, a young people, not possessed of full powers of reflection, needed around it, so to say, a people that had in it more of the forces of death. In overcoming another people, it won through to what it needed for its own evolution.

And so we find that these Oriental conflicts, often so terrible and presenting to us such a barbarous aspect, are in reality nothing else than the impulses of human evolution. They had to take place. Mankind would not have been able to develop on the earth, had it not been for these terrible wars and struggles that seem to us so barbarous.

Already in those olden times the Initiates of the Mysteries saw the world as it is seen to-day. Only they united with this perception a different attitude of mind and soul. For them, all that they experienced in clear, sharp outlines— even as we to-day experience external objects in sharp outlines, when we perceive with our senses—was something that came from the Gods, that came even for human consciousness from the Gods. For how did external objects present themselves to an Initiate of those times ? There was perhaps a flash of lightning (to take a simple and obvious illustration). You know very well what a flash of lightning

32

looks like to a man of to-day. The men of olden time did not see it thus. They saw living spiritual Beings moving in the sky, and the sharp line of the flash disappeared completely. They saw a host, a procession of spiritual Beings hurrying forward over or in cosmic space. The lightning as such they did not see. They saw a host of spirits hovering and moving through cosmic space.

The Initiate also saw, with the rest, this spiritual host, but he had developed within him the perception that we have to-day, and so for him, the picture began to grow dim and the heavenly host gradually disappeared from view, and then the flash of lightning could become manifest.

The whole of Nature, in the form in which we see it to-day, could only be attained in olden times through initiation. But how did man feel towards such knowledge? He did not by any means look on the knowledge thus attained with the indifference with which knowledge and truth are regarded to-day. There was a strong moral element in man's experience of knowledge. If we turn our gaze to what happened with the neophytes of the Mysteries, we find we have to describe it in the following way. When a few individuals, after undergoing severe inner tests and trials, had been initiated into the view of Nature, which to-day is accessible to all, they had quite naturally this feeling : consider the man with his ordinary consciousness. He sees the host of elementary beings riding through the air. But just because he has such a perception, he is devoid of free will. He is entirely given up to the Divine-spiritual world. For in this waking-dreaming, dreaming-waking, the will does not move in freedom, rather is it something that streams into man as Divine will. And the Initiate, who saw the lightning come forth out of these Imaginations, learned to say : I must be a man who is free to move in the world *without* the Gods, one for whom the Gods cast out the world-content into the void.

Now you must understand, this condition would have been unbearable for the Initiate, had there not been for him moments that compensated for it. Such moments he did have. For while on the one hand the Initiate learned to experience Asia as God-forsaken, Spirit-forsaken, he learned also to know a still deeper state of consciousness than that which reached up to the Second Hierarchy. Knowing the world bereft of God, he learned also to know the world of the Seraphim, Cherubim and Thrones.

At a certain time in the epoch of Asiatic evolution, approximately in the middle—later on we shall have to speak more exactly of the dates—the condition of consciousness of the Initiates was such that they went about on Earth with very nearly the perception of the kingdoms of the Earth which is possessed by modern man ; they felt it, however, in their limbs. They felt their limbs set free from the Gods in a God-bereft earthly substance.

In compensation for this, however, they met in this godless land the high Gods of the Seraphim, Cherubim and Thrones. As Initiates they learned to know, no longer the grey-green spiritual Beings that were the Pictures of the forest, the Pictures of the trees, they learned as Initiates to know the forest devoid of Spirit. Theirs, however, was the compensation of meeting in the forest Beings of the First Hierarchy, there they would meet some Being from the Kingdom of the Seraphim, Cherubim and Thrones.

All this, understood as giving form to the social life of humanity, is the essential feature in the historical evolution of the ancient East. And the driving force for further evolution lies in the search for an adjustment between young races and old races, so that the young races may mature through association with the old, with the souls of those whom they have brought into subjection. However far back we look into Asia, everywhere we find how the young races who cannot of themselves develop the reflective faculties, set out to find these in wars of aggression.

When, however, we turn our gaze away from Asia to the land of Greece, we find a somewhat different development. Over in Greece, in the time of the full flower of Greek culture, we find a people who did indeed know how to grow old, but were unable to permeate the growing old with full spirituality. I have many times had to draw attention to the characteristic Greek utterance : **Better a beggar in the world of the living than a king in the realm of the shades.** Neither to death outside in Nature, nor to death in man, could the Greek adapt himself. He could not find his true relation with death. On the other hand, however, he had this death within him. And so in the Greek we find, not a longing for a reflective consciousness, but apprehension and fear of death.

Such a fear of death was not felt by the young Eastern races ; *they* went out to make conquests, when as a race they found themselves unable to experience death in the right way. The inner conflict, however, which the Greeks experienced with death became in its turn an inner impulse compelling humanity, and led to what we know as the Trojan War. The Greeks had no need to seek death at the hands of a foreign race in order to acquire the power of reflection. The Greeks needed to come into a right relation with what they felt and experienced of death, they needed to find the inner living mystery of death. And this led to that great conflict between the Greeks and the people in Asia from whom they had originated. The Trojan war is a war of sorrow, a war of apprehension and fear. We see facing one another the Greeks, who felt death within them but did not know, as it were, what to do with it, and the Oriental races who were bent on conquest, who wanted death and had it not. The Greeks had death, but were at a loss how to adapt themselves to it. They needed the infusion of another element, before they could discover its secret. Achilles, Agamemnon—all these men bore death within them, but could not adapt themselves to it. They look across to Asia. There in Asia they see a people who are in the reverse position, who are suffering under the direct influence of the opposite condition. Over there are men who do not feel death in the intense way it is felt by the Greeks themselves, over there are men to whom death is something abounding in life.

All this has been brought to expression in a wonderful way by Homer. Wherever he sets the Trojans over against

35

the Greeks, everywhere he lets us see this contrast. You may see it, for instance, in the characteristic figures of Hector and Achilles. And in this contrast is expressed what is taking place on the frontier of Asia and Europe. Asia, in those olden times, had, as it were, a superabundance of life over death, yearned after death. Europe had, on the Greek soil, a superabundance of death in man, and man was at a loss to find his true relation to it. Thus from a second point of view we see Europe and Asia set over against one another.

In the first place, we had the transition from rhythmic memory to temporal memory ; now we have these two quite different experiences in respect of death in the human organisation. To-morrow we will consider more in detail the contrast, which I have only been able to indicate at the close of to-day's lecture, and so approach a fuller understanding of the transitions that lead over from Asia to Europe. For these had a deep and powerful influence on the evolution of man, and without understanding them we can really arrive at no understanding of the evolution we are passing through at the present day.

III

THIRTEEN YEARS AGO, almost to the day, in a course of lectures that I gave in Stuttgart between Christmas and New Year, I spoke of the same events that we shall treat of in the present course of lectures. Only we shall have to alter the standpoint somewhat. In the first two introductory lectures we have been at pains to acquire an understanding for the radical change in man's life of thought and feeling that has come about in the course of human evolution, prehistoric as well as historic. In to-day's lecture, at any rate to begin with, we shall not need to go back more than a few thousand years.

You know that from the standpoint of Spiritual Science we have to regard as of paramount importance in its consequences for human evolution the so-called Atlantean catastrophe which befell the Earth in the time commonly known as the later Ice Age. It was the last Act in the downfall of the Atlantean continent, which continent forms to-day the floor of the Atlantic Ocean ; and following it we have as we have often described, five great successive epochs of civilisation, leading up to our own time. Of the two earliest of these we have no trace in historical tradition, for the literature remaining in the East, even all that is contained in the magnificent Vedas, in the profound Vedantic philosophy, is but an echo of what we should have to describe, if we wanted to recall these ancient epochs. In my *Outline of Occult Science* I have always spoken of them as the Ancient Indian and the Ancient Persian.

To-day we shall not have to go so far back as this ; we will direct our thoughts to the period which I have often designated as the Egypto-Chaldean, the period preceding the Graeco-Latin. We have already had to draw attention

37

to the fact that during the time between the Atlantean catastrophe and the Greek period, great changes took place in regard to man's power of memory and also in regard to the social life of humanity. A memory such as we have to-day—the temporal memory, by means of which we can take ourselves back in time—was not in existence in this third Post-Atlantean period ; man had then, as we have described in an earlier lecture, a memory that was linked to rhythmic experience. And we have seen how this rhythmic memory proceeded from a still earlier memory that was particularly strong in the Atlantean period, namely, the localised memory, where man only bore within him a consciousness of the present, but used all manner of things which he found in the external world or which he himself set there, as memorials by means of which he put himself into relationship with the past ; and not alone with his own personal past, but with the past of humanity in general.

In this connection we have not only to think of memorials that were on the Earth ; in those ancient times the constellations in the heavens served man as memorials, especially in their recurrences and in the variations of these recurrences. From the constellations man perceived how things were in earlier times. Thus did heaven and earth work together to build for an ancient humanity the localised memory.

Now the man of long past times was different in the whole constitution of his being from the man of a later time, and still more so from the man of our own time. Man to-day, in his waking condition, bears the Ego and astral body within him unnoticed, as it were ; most people do not notice how the physical bears within it, along with the etheric body, a much more important organisation than itself, namely, the astral body and the Ego-organisation. You, of course, are familiar with these connections. But an ancient humanity felt this fact of their own being quite differently.

And it is to such a humanity that we must return, when we go back to the third epoch of Post-Atlantean civilisation, —the Egypto-Chaldean. At that time man experienced himself as spirit and soul still to a great extent outside his physical and etheric body, even when awake. He knew how to distinguish : This I have as my spirit and soul,—we, of course, call it the Ego and the astral body—and it is linked with my physical body and my etheric body. He went through the world in this experience of twofoldness. He did not call his physical and his etheric body ' I.' He called ' I ' only his soul and spirit, that which was spiritual and was in a manner connected downward with his physical and etheric bodies, had a connection with them that he could observe and feel. And in this spirit and soul, in this Ego and astral body, man was made aware of the entry of the Divine-spiritual Hierarchies, even as to-day he feels the entry of natural substances into his physical body.

To-day man's experience in the physical body is of the following nature. He knows that with the process of nourishment, with the process of breathing, he receives the substances of the external kingdoms of Nature. Before, they are outside ; then they are within him. They enter him, penetrate him and become part of him. In that earlier age, when man experienced a certain separation of his soul-and-spirit nature from his physical and etheric nature, he knew that Angels, Archangels and other Beings up to the highest Hierarchies are themselves spiritual substance that penetrates his soul and spirit and becomes—if I may put it so—part of him. So that at every moment of life he was able to say : In me live the Gods. And he looked upon his Ego, not as built up from below by means of physical and etheric substances, but as bestowed on him through grace from above, as coming from the Hierarchies. And as a burden, or rather as a vehicle, in which he feels himself borne forward in the physical world as in a vehicle of life— so did he conceive of his physical-etheric nature. Until this is clearly grasped, we shall not understand the course of events in the evolution of mankind.

We could trace this course of events by reference to many different examples. To-day we will follow one thread, the same that I touched upon thirteen years ago, when I spoke of

39

that historic document which represents the most ancient phase of the evolution we have now to consider,—I mean, the Epic of Gilgamish.

The Epic of Gilgamish has in part the character of a Saga, and so to-day I will set before you the events that I described thirteen years ago, as they manifest themselves directly to spiritual vision.

In a certain town in Asia Minor—it is called Erech in the Epic—there lived a man who belonged to the conquering type of which we spoke in the last lecture, the type that sprang so truly and naturally out of the whole mental and social conditions of the time. The Epic calls him Gilgamish. We have then to do with a personality who has preserved many characteristics of the humanity of earlier times. Clear though it is, however, to this personality that he has, as it were, a dual nature,—that he has on the one hand the spirit-and-soul nature into which the Gods descend, and on the other hand, the physical-and-etheric into which substances of the Earth and the Cosmos, physical and etheric substances, enter, —it is none the less a fact that the representative people of his time are already passing through a transition into a later stage of human evolution. The transition consisted in this. The Ego-consciousness, which a comparatively short time previously was above in the sphere of spirit and soul, had now, if I may so express it, sunk down into the physical and etheric, so that Gilgamish was one of those who began no longer to say ' I ' to the spirit-and-soul part of their being, in which they felt the presence of the Gods, but to say ' I ' to that which was earthly and etheric in them. Such was the stage of development in the human soul life of that time.

But along with this condition of soul, where the Ego has drawn down from the spirit and soul and entered as conscious Ego into the bodily and etheric, this personality had still left in him habits belonging to the past ; and especially the habit of experiencing memory solely in connection with rhythm. He still retained also that inward feeling that one must learn to know the forces of death, because the death-forces can alone give to man that which brings him to powers of reflection.

Now owing to the fact that in the personality of Gilgamish we have to do with a soul who had already gone through many incarnations on Earth and had now entered into the new form of human existence which I have just described, we find him at this point in a physical existence that bore in it a strain of uncertainty. The justification, as it were, of the habits of conquest, the justification, too, of the rhythmic memory, were beginning to lose their validity for the Earth. And so the experiences of Gilgamish were throughout the experiences of an age of transition.

Hence it came about that when this personality, in accordance with the old custom, conquered and seized the city that in the Epic is called Erech, dissensions arose in the city. At first he was not liked. He was regarded as a foreigner and indeed would never have been able alone to meet all the difficulties that presented themselves in consequence of his capture of the city. Then there appeared, because destiny had led him thither, another personality— the Epic of Gilgamish calls him Eabani—a personality who had descended relatively late to the Earth from that planetary existence which Earth-humanity led for a period, as you will find described in my *Outline of Occult Science*.

You know how during the Atlantean epoch souls descended, some earlier, some later, from the different planets, having withdrawn thither from the Earth at a very early stage of Earth evolution.

In Gilgamish we have to do with an individuality, who returned comparatively early to the Earth ; thus at the time of which we are speaking he had already experienced many Earth incarnations.

In the other individuality who had now also come to that city we have to do with one who had remained comparatively long in planetary existence and only later found his way back to Earth. You may read of this from a somewhat different point of view in my Stuttgart lectures of thirteen years ago.

41

Now this second individuality formed an intimate friendship with Gilgamish ; and together they were able to establish the social life of the city on a really permanent footing. This was possible because there remained to this second personality a great deal of the knowledge that came from that sojourn in the Cosmos beyond the Earth, and that was preserved for a few incarnations after the return to Earth. He had, as I said in Stuttgart, a kind of enlightened cognition ; clairvoyance, clairaudience and what we may call clair-cognition. Thus we have in the one personality what remained of the old habits of conquest and of the rhythmically-directed memory, and in the other what remained to him from vision and penetration into the secret mysteries of the Cosmos. And from the flowing together of these two things, there grew up, as was indeed generally the case in those olden times, the whole social structure of that city in Asia Minor. Peace and happiness descended upon the city and its inhabitants, and everything would have been in order, had not a certain event taken place that set the whole course of affairs in another direction.

There was in that city a Mystery, the Mystery of a Goddess, and this Mystery preserved very many secrets relating to the Cosmos. It was, however, in the meaning of those times, what I may call a kind of synthetic Mystery. That is to say, in this Mystery revelations were collected together from various Mysteries of Asia. And the contents of these Mysteries were cultivated and taught there in diverse ways at different times. Now this was not easily understood by the personality who bears the name of Gilgamish in the Epic, and he made complaint against the Mystery that its teachings were contradictory. And seeing that the two personalities of whom we are speaking were those who really held the whole ordering of the city in their hands and that complaints against the Mystery came from so important a quarter, trouble ensued ; and at length things became so difficult that the priests of the Mysteries appealed to those Powers Who in former times were accessible to man in the Mysteries. It will not surprise you to hear that in the ancient Mysteries man could actually address himself to the Spiritual Beings of the higher Hierarchies ; for, as I told you yesterday, to the ancient Oriental, Asia was none else than the lowest heaven and in this lowest heaven man was aware of the presence of Divine-spiritual Beings and had intercourse with them. Such intercourse was especially cultivated in the Mysteries. And so the priests of the Istar Mysteries turned to those Spiritual Powers to whom they always turned when they sought enlightenment ; and it came about that these Spiritual Powers inflicted a certain punishment upon the city.

What happened was expressed at the time in the following way : Something that is really a higher spiritual force, is working in Erech as an animal power, as a terrible spectral animal power. Trouble of all kinds befell the inhabitants, physical illnesses and more especially diseases and disturbances of the soul. The consequence was that the personality who had attached himself to Gilgamish and who is called Eabani in the Epic, died ; but in order that the mission of the other personality might be continued on Earth, he remained with this personality spiritually, even after death. Thus when we consider the later life and development of the personality who in the Epic bears the name of Gilgamish, we have still to see in it the working together in the two personalities ; but now in such a way that in the subsequent years of Gilgamish's life he receives intuitions and enlightenment from Eabani, and so continues to act, although alone, not simply out of his own will, but out of the will of both, from the flowing together of the will of both.

What I have here placed before you is something that was fully possible in those olden times. Man's life of thought and feeling was not then so single and united as it is to-day. Hence it could not have the experience of freedom, in the sense in which we know it to-day. It was quite possible, either for a spiritual Being who had never incarnated on Earth to work through the will of an earthly personality, or, as was the case here, for a human personality who had passed through death and was living an after-death existence,

43

to speak and act through the will of a personality on Earth. So it was with Gilgamish. And from what resulted in this way through the flowing together of the two wills, Gilgamish was able to recognise with considerable clearness at what point he himself stood in the history of mankind. Through the influence of the spirit that inspired him, he began to know that the Ego had sunk down into the physical body and etheric body,—which are mortal ; and from that moment the problem of immortality began to play an intensely strong part in his life. His whole longing was set on finding his way by some means or other into the very heart of this problem. The Mysteries, wherein was preserved what there was to say on Earth in those days concerning immortality, did not readily reveal their secrets to Gilgamish. The Mysteries had still their tradition, and in their tradition was preserved also in great measure the living knowledge that was present on Earth in Atlantean times, when the ancient original wisdom ruled among men.

The bearers of this original wisdom, however, who once went about on Earth as Spiritual Beings, had long ago withdrawn and founded the cosmic colony of the Moon. For it is pure childishness to suppose that the Moon is the dead frozen body that modern physics describes. The Moon is, before all, the cosmic world of those Spiritual Beings Who were the first great teachers of earthly humanity, the Beings Who once brought to earthly humanity the primeval wisdom and Who, when the Moon had left the Earth and sought a place for itself in the planetary system, withdrew also and took up their abode on this Moon.

He who to-day through Imaginative cognition is able to attain to a true knowledge of the Moon, gains knowledge too of the Spiritual Beings in this cosmic colony, Who were once the teachers of the ancient wisdom to humanity on Earth. What they had taught was preserved in the Mysteries, and also the impulses whereby man himself is able to come into a certain relationship with this ancient wisdom.

The personality who is called Gilgamish in the Epic had, however, no living connection with these Mysteries of Asia

44

Minor. But through the supersensible influence of the friend who, in the after-death existence, was still united with him, there arose in Gilgamish an inner impulse to seek out paths in the world whereby he might be able to come to an experience concerning the immortality of the soul. Later on, in the Middle Ages, when man desired to learn something concerning the spiritual world, he would sink down into his own inner being. In more modern times one could say that a still more inward process is followed. In those olden times, however, of which we are speaking, it was a matter of clear and exact knowledge to man that the Earth is not the mere lump of rock which the geology books would lead one to imagine, but that the Earth is a living being,—a living being, moreover, endowed with soul and spirit. As a tiny insect that runs over a human being may learn something of that human being as it passes over his nose and forehead, or through his hair, as the insect acquires its knowledge in this way by making a journey over the human being, so in those times it was by setting forth upon journeys over the Earth and by learning to know the Earth with its different configurations in different places, that man gained insight into the spiritual world. And this he was able to do, whether access to the Mysteries were permitted to him or no. It is in truth no mere superficial account that relates how Pythagoras and others wandered far and wide in order to attain their knowledge. Men went about the Earth in order to receive what was revealed in its manifold configurations, in all that they could observe from the different forms and shapes of the Earth in different places; and not of the Earth in its physical aspect alone, but of the Earth too as soul and spirit.

To-day men may travel to Africa, to Italy,—and yet, with the exception of external details, at which they gape and stare, their experience in these places may be very little different from their experience at home. For man's sensitiveness to the deep differences that subsist between different places of the Earth has gone.

In the period with which we are now dealing, it had not died out. Thus the impulse to wander over the Earth and thereby receive something that should help to the solution of the problem of immortality, betokened something full of meaning for Gilgamish.

So he set forth upon his wanderings. And they had for him a result that was of very great significance. He came to a region that is nearly the same as we now call Burgenland, a district much talked of in recent times and concerning which there has been a good deal of contention as to whether it should belong to Hungary or not. The whole social conditions of the country have of course greatly changed since those far off times. Gilgamish came thither and found there an ancient Mystery—the High Priest of the Mystery is called Xisuthros in the Epic—an ancient Mystery that was a genuine successor, as it were, of the old Atlantean Mysteries ; only, of course, in a changed form, as must of necessity be the case after so long a time had elapsed.

And it was so that in this ancient Mystery centre they knew how to judge and appraise the faculty of knowledge that Gilgamish possessed. He was met with understanding. A test was imposed upon him, one that in those days was often imposed on pupils of the Mysteries. He had to go through certain exercises, wide-awake, for seven days and seven nights. It was too much for him, so he submitted himself only to the substitute or alternative for the test. Certain substances were made ready for him, of which he then partook, and by means of them received a certain enlightenment ; although, as is always the case when certain exceptional conditions are not assured, the enlightenment might be doubtful in some respects. Nevertheless a degree of enlightenment was there, a certain insight into the great connections in the Universe, into the spiritual structure of the Universe. And so, when Gilgamish had ended his wandering and was returning home again, he did in fact possess a high spiritual insight.

He travelled along the Danube, following the river on its northern bank, until he came again to his home, to the home of his choice. But before he reached home, because he did not receive the initiation into the Post-Atlantean

46

Mystery in the other way that I described, but instead in a somewhat uncertain way, he succumbed to the first temptation that assailed him and fell into a terrible fit of anger over an event that came to his notice,—something, in effect, which he heard had taken place in the city. He heard of the event before he reached the city, and burst out into a storm of anger ; and in consequence, the enlightenment he had received was almost entirely darkened, so that he arrived home without it.

Nevertheless,—and this is the peculiar characteristic of this personality—he still had the possibility, through the connection with the spirit of his dead friend, of looking into the spiritual world, or at least of receiving information thence.

It is, however, one thing by means of an initiation to acquire direct vision into the spiritual world, and another thing to receive information from a personality who is in the after-death condition. Still, we may say with truth that something of an insight into the nature of immortality did remain with Gilgamish. I am setting aside just now the experiences that are undergone by man after death ; these do not yet play very strongly into the consciousness of the next incarnation, nor did they in those days ;—into the life, into the inner constitution they do work very strongly, but not into the consciousness.

You now have before you these two personalities whom I have described and who together bring to expression the mental and spiritual constitution of man in the third Post-Atlantean period of civilisation at about the middle point of its development,—two personalities who still lived in such a way that the whole manner of their life was in itself strong evidence of the duality in man's nature. The one— Gilgamish—was conscious of this duality ; he was one of the first to experience the descent of the Ego-consciousness, the descent of the Ego into the physical and etheric nature in man. The other, inasmuch as he had passed through but few incarnations on Earth, had a clairvoyant knowledge, by means of which he was able to know that there is no such thing as matter, but that everything is spiritual and the so-called material only another form of the spiritual.

Now you can imagine that, if a man's being were so constituted, he could certainly not think and feel what we think and feel to-day. His whole thinking and feeling was indeed totally different from ours. And what such personalities could receive in the way of instruction was of course quite unlike what is taught to-day at school or in the universities. Everything of a spiritual or cultural nature that men received in those days came to them from the Mysteries, whence it was spread abroad as widely as possible among men by all manner of channels. It was the wise men, the priests, in the Mysteries, who were the true teachers of humanity.

Now it was characteristic of these two personalities that in the incarnation that we have described they were unable just because of their special constitution of soul, to approach the Mysteries of their own land. The one who is named Eabani in the Epic stood near the Mysteries through his sojourn in the extra-earthly regions of the Cosmos ; the one who is named Gilgamish experienced a kind of initiation in a Post-Atlantean Mystery, which however only bore half fruit in him. The result of all this was that both felt in their own being, as it were, something that made them kin to the primeval times of earthly humanity. Both were able to put the question to themselves : How have we become what we are ? What share have we had in the evolution of the Earth ? We have become what we are through the evolution of the Earth ; what part have we played in its evolution ?

The question of immortality that was the occasion of such suffering and conflict to Gilgamish, was connected in those days with a necessary vision into the evolution of the Earth in primeval times. One could not think or feel—using the words in the sense of those times—about the immortality of the soul unless one had at the same time some vision of how human souls who were already there in very early phases of the Earth's evolution, during the Ancient Sun and Ancient Moon embodiments, saw approaching them, that which later

48

has become what we call earthly. Men felt they belonged to the Earth. They felt that to know himself, man must behold and recognise his connection with the Earth.

Now the secret knowledge that was cultivated in all Mysteries of Asia, was first and foremost cosmic knowledge ; its wisdom and its teachings unfolded the origin of the evolution of the Earth in connection with the Cosmos. So that in these Mysteries there appeared before men in a living way, in such a way that it could become living Ideas in them, a far-spread vision, showing them how the Earth evolved, and how in the heave and surge of the substances and forces of the Earth, all through the Sun, Moon and Earth periods of evolution, man has been evolving together with all these substances. All this was set before men in a most vivid manner.

One of the Mysteries where such things were taught, was continued on into much later times. It was the Mystery centre of Ephesus. This Mystery had in the very middle of its sanctuary the image of the Goddess Artemis. When we look to-day at pictures of the goddess Artemis, we have perhaps only the grotesque impression of a female form with many breasts. This is because we have no idea how such things were experienced in olden times; and it was the inner experience evoked by these things that was all-important. The pupils of the Mysteries had to go through a certain preparation before they were conducted to the true centre of the Mysteries. In the Ephesian Mysteries the centre was this image of the Goddess Artemis. When the pupil was led up to the centre, he became one with such an image. As he stood before the image, he lost the consciousness that he was there in front of it, enclosed in his skin. He acquired the consciousness that he himself is what the image is. He identified himself with the image. This identification of himself in consciousness with the divine image at Ephesus had the following effect. The pupil no longer merely looked out upon the kingdoms of the Earth that were round about him—the stones, trees, rivers, clouds and so forth—but when he felt himself one with the image, when he entered as it were into the image of Artemis, he received an inner vision of his connection with the kingdoms of the Ether. He felt himself one with the world of the stars, one with the processes in the world of the stars. He did not feel himself as earthly substance within a human skin, he felt his cosmic existence. He felt himself in the etheric. And as he did so, there rose before him earlier conditions of Earth-experience and of man's experience on Earth. He began to see what these earlier conditions had been. To-day we look upon the Earth as a great piece of rock or stone, covered with water over a large part of its surface and surrounded by a sphere of air containing oxygen and nitrogen and other substances,—containing, in fact, what the human being requires for breathing. And so on and so on. And when men begin to explain and speculate on what passes to-day for scientific knowledge, then we get a fine result indeed ! For only by means of spiritual vision can one penetrate to the conditions that prevailed in the earliest primeval times. Such a spiritual vision, however, concerning primeval conditions of the Earth and of mankind was attained by the pupils of Ephesus, when they identified themselves with the divine image ; they beheld and understood how formerly what surrounds the Earth to-day as atmosphere was not as it now is ; surrounding the Earth, in the place where the atmosphere is to-day, was an extraordinarily fine albumen, a volatile, fluid albuminous substance. And they saw how everything that lived on the Earth required for its own genesis the forces of this volatile, fluid albuminous substance, that was spread over the Earth, and how everything also lived in it. They saw too how that which was in a certain sense already within this substance—finely distributed but everywhere with a tendency to crystallisation—how that which was present in a finely distributed condition as silicic acid was in reality a kind of sense-organ for the Earth and could take up into itself from all sides the Imaginations and influences from the surrounding Cosmos. And thus in the silicic acid contained in the earthly albuminous atmosphere were everywhere Imaginations, concretely, externally present.

These Imaginations had the form of gigantic, plant-like organisms, and out of that which was, so to speak, ' imagined ' into the Earth in this way, there developed later, through absorption of the atmospheric substance,— the plant ; everything that is of a plantlike nature. At first it was in the environment of the Earth, in volatile, fluid form ; only later did it sink down into the soil and become what is known to us as the plant.

Besides the silicic acid, there was imbedded also in this albumen-atmosphere another substance, lime, in a finely-divided condition. Again, out of the lime substance, under the influence of the congelation of the albumen there arose the animal kingdom. And the human being felt himself within all this. He felt one with the whole Earth. He lived in that which formed itself as plant in the Earth through Imagination, he lived too in that which was developing on Earth as animal, in the way I have described. Each single human being felt himself spread out over the whole Earth, felt himself one with the Earth. So that the human beings were all—as I have described it for the Platonic teaching in my book *Christianity as Mystical Fact*, in reference to the human capacity for ideas—were all each within the other.

Now destiny brought it about that the two personalities, of whom I spoke in Stuttgart and of whom I am speaking to you again here, reincarnated as adherents of the Mystery of Ephesus, and there received with deep devotion into their souls the things that I have here pictured to you in brief outline. Thereby their souls were, in a manner, inwardly established. Through the Mystery they now received as Earth-wisdom what had formerly been accessible to them only in experience,—for the most part unconscious experience.

Thus was the human experience of these personalities divided between two separate incarnations. And thereby did they bear within them a strong consciousness of man's connection with the higher, the spiritual world, and at the same time a strong, an intense capacity for feeling and experiencing all that belongs to the Earth.

For if you have two things that perpetually flow together, so that you cannot keep them apart, then they merge and lose themselves in each other. If, on the other hand, they show themselves clearly distinct, then you can judge the one by the other. And so these two personalities were able on the one hand to judge the spiritual of the higher world that came to them as a result of life-experience and that lived in them as an echo from their earlier incarnations. And now, as the origin of the kingdoms of nature was communicated to them in the Mystery of Ephesus under the influence of the Goddess Artemis, they were able, on the other hand, to judge how the things external to man on the Earth came into being, how gradually everything external to man on the Earth was formed out of a primeval substance, which substance also included man. And the life of these two personalities—it fell partly in the latter end of the time when Heraclitus was still living in Ephesus, and partly in the time that followed—became particularly rich inwardly and was powerfully lit up from within with the light of great cosmic secrets. There was in them moreover a strong consciousness of how man in his life of soul may be connected, not merely with that which lies spread out around him on the Earth, but with that too which extends upward,—when he himself reaches upward with his being. Such was the inner configuration of soul of these two personalities, who had worked together in the earlier Egypto-Chaldean epoch and then lived together at the time of Heraclitus and after, in connection with the Mystery of Ephesus. And now this working together was able to continue still further. The configuration of soul that had been developed in both, passed through death, through the spiritual world, and began to prepare itself for an Earth life that must needs again bring problems which will now of course present themselves in quite a different way. And when we observe in what manner these two personalities had to find their part later in the history of Earth evolution, we may see how through the experiences of the soul in earlier times—these experiences having their karmic continuation in the next life on Earth—things are prepared which afterwards appear in totally different form in the later life, when the personalities are once more incorporated into the evolution of humanity on Earth.

I have brought forward this example, because these two personalities make their appearance later in a period that was of extraordinary importance in the history of mankind. I indicated this in my lectures at Stuttgart thirteen years ago ; in fact, I dealt with all these matters from a certain point of view. These personalities who had first in the Egypto-Chaldean epoch gone through what I may call a widely-extended cosmic life, and had then deepened this cosmic experience within them, thereby in a sense establishing their souls, now lived again in a later incarnation as Aristotle and Alexander the Great. When one understands the underlying depths in the souls of Aristotle and Alexander the Great, then one can begin to understand, as I explained in Stuttgart, all that was working so problematically in these two personalities, whose lives took their course in the time when Greek culture was falling into decay and Roman rule beginning to have dominion.

IV

IT WAS MY TASK YESTERDAY to show from the example of individual personalities how the historical evolution of the world runs its course. If one seeks to come further in the direction of Spiritual Science, one cannot represent things otherwise than by showing the consequences of events as they reflect themselves in the human being. For not until our own epoch does man feel himself for reasons which we will discuss in the course of these lectures, shut off as an individual being from the rest of the world. In all previous epochs man felt—and, be it noted, in all subsequent epochs man will again feel himself as member of the whole Cosmos, as belonging to the entire world ; even as a finger (as I have often expressed it) can have no independent existence for itself, but can only exist on a human being. For the moment a finger is separated from the human being, it is no longer a finger, it begins to decay, it is something quite different, subject to quite other laws than when attached to the human organism. And as a finger is only a finger in unison with the organism, so in the same way is man only a being having some form or other, whether in Earth-life or in the life between death and a new birth, in connection with the entire Cosmos. The consciousness of this was present in earlier epochs and will again be present in a later time ; it is only darkened to-day because, as we shall hear, it was necessary for man that it should be darkened and clouded in order that he might develop to the full the experience of freedom. The farther we go back however into ancient times, the more do we find man possessing this consciousness of belonging to the whole Cosmos.

I have given you a picture of two personalities,—the one called Gilgamish in the famous Epic and the other Eabani.

55

I have shown you how these personalities lived in the ancient Egypto-Chaldean epoch in accordance with what was possible to men of that time, and how they afterwards experienced a deepening through the Mysteries of Ephesus. And I told you at the end of my lecture yesterday that these same human beings had their part later in the historical evolution of the world as Aristotle and Alexander.

In order now fully to understand the course of Earth evolution in the times when all these things were taking place, we must look more closely into what such souls were able to receive into themselves in these three successive periods.

I have told you how the personality who is concealed behind the name of Gilgamish undertook a journey to the West and went through a kind of Western Post-Atlantean initiation.

Let us first form an idea of the nature of such an initiation, that we may the better understand what came later. We shall naturally turn to a place where echoes of the old Atlantean initiation remained on for a long time. This was the case with the Hibernian Mysteries, of which I have recently spoken to the friends who are here in Dornach. I must now repeat some of what I then said before we can come to a clear and full understanding of the subject we are treating.

The Mysteries of Hibernia, the Irish Mysteries, were in existence for a long time. They were still there at the time of the foundation of Christianity. And they are the Mysteries that in some respects preserved most faithfully the ancient wisdom-teaching of the Atlantean peoples. Let me give you a picture of the experiences of a person who was initiated into the Irish Mysteries in the Post-Atlantean epoch. Before he was able to receive the initiation he had to be strictly prepared ; the preparation that had to be undergone before entering the Mysteries was always in those times of extraordinary strictness and rigour. The important thing in the Hibernian Mysteries was that the pupil should learn to become aware in powerful inward experience of

that which is *illusory* in his environment,—in all the things,
that is to say, to which man attributes being on the ground
of his sense-perception. Then he was made aware of all
the difficulties and obstacles which meet man when he
searches after the *truth*, the real truth. And he was shown
how, fundamentally, everything which surrounds us in the
world of the senses is an illusion, that what the senses give
is illusion, and that the truth conceals itself behind the
illusion, so that in fact true being is not accessible to man
through sense-perception.

Now, very likely you will say that this conviction you
yourselves have held for a long time ; you know this quite
well. But all the knowledge a man can have in the present-
day consciousness of the illusory character of the sense-
world is as nothing compared with the inner shattering,
the inner tragedy that men of that time suffered in their
preparation for the Hibernian initiation. For when one
says theoretically in this way : Everything is Maya, everything is illusion,—one takes it quite lightly ! But the training of the Hibernian pupils was carried to such a point that
they had to say to themselves : There is for man no possibility
of penetrating the illusion and coming to real true Being.

The pupils were by this means trained to content themselves, as it were in desperation, with the illusion. They
came into an attitude of despair : the illusory character,
they felt, is so overpowering and so penetrating that one
can never get beyond it. And in the life of these pupils
we find always the feeling : Very well then, we must remain
in the illusion. That means, however : we must lose the
very ground from under our feet. For there is no standing
firm on illusion ! In truth, my dear friends, of the strictness
and severity of the preparation in the ancient Mysteries,
we to-day can scarcely form any idea. Men shrink in
terror before what inner development actually demands.

Such was the experience that came to the pupils in regard
to Being and its illusory character. And now there awaited
them a similar experience regarding the search after Truth.
They learned to know the hindrances man has in his emotions

57

that hinder him from coming to truth, all the dark and over-whelming feelings that trouble the clear light of knowledge. And so once more they came to a great moment when they said to themselves : If Truth is not, well then we live—we must live—in error, in untruth. For a man to come thus to a time in his life when he despairs of Being and of Truth means, in short, that he tears out of him his own humanity.

All this was given in order that the human being, through experiencing the opposite of what he was finally to reach as his goal, might approach that goal with the right and deep human feeling. For unless one has learned what it means to live with error and illusion, then one cannot value Being and Truth. And the pupils of Hibernia had to learn to value Being and Truth.

And then, when they had gone through all this, when they had, as it were, experienced to the bitter end, the opposite pole of what they were eventually to reach, the pupils were led (and here I must describe what happened in the picture-language that can rightly represent what took place as reality in the Hibernian Mysteries)—they were led into a kind of sanctuary where were two pillar-statues of infinitely strong suggestive force, and of gigantic size. The one of these pillar-statues was inwardly hollow ; the surface that sur-rounded the hollow space, the whole substance, that is, of which the statue consisted, was elastic throughout. Where-ever one pressed, one could make an indentation into the statue ; but the moment one ceased to press, the form restored itself.

The whole pillar-statue was made in such a way that the head was more particularly developed. When a man approached the statue, he had the feeling : Forces are stream-ing forth from the head into the colossal body. For of course he did not see the space within, he only became aware of it when he pressed. And the pupil was exhorted to press. He had the feeling that the forces of the head rayed out over the whole of the rest of the body, that in this statue the head does everything.

I willingly admit, my dear friends, that if a modern man in our present-day prosaic life were led before the statue, he would scarcely be able to experience anything but quite abstract ideas about it. That is certainly so. But it is a different matter, first to experience with one's whole inner being, with soul and spirit, yes, and with blood and nerves, the might of illusion and the might of error,—and then, after that, to experience the suggestive force of such a gigantic figure.

This statue had a male character.

By the side of it stood another, that had a female character. It was not hollow. It was composed of a substance that was not elastic, but plastic. When the pupil pressed this statue—and again he was exhorted to do so—he destroyed the form. He dug a hole in the body.

After the pupil had found how in the one statue, owing to its elasticity, the form was always re-established, and how in the other he defaced the statue by pressing it, and after something else too had taken place, of which I shall speak presently, he left the place, and was only led back there again when all the deformations he had caused in the plastic non-elastic female figure had been restored, and the statue was intact. Thanks to all the preparations which the pupil had undergone—and I can only give them here in outline—he was able to receive in connection with the statue having a female character a deep inner experience in the whole of his being—body, soul and spirit.

This inner experience had of course been already prepared in him earlier, but it was established and confirmed in full measure through the suggestive influence of the statue. He received into him a feeling of inward numbness, of hard and frozen numbness. This so worked in him that he saw his soul filled with Imaginations. And these Imaginations were pictures of the Earth's winter, pictures that represented the winter of the Earth. Thus was the pupil led to perceive Reality, in the spirit, from within.

With the other, the male statue, he had a different experience. He felt as though all the life in him, which was generally spread out over the whole body, went into his blood, as if his blood were permeated with forces and pressing against his skin. Whereas before the one statue he had to feel that he was becoming a frozen skeleton, he had now to feel before the other that all the life in him was being consumed in heat, and he was living in a tightly-stretched skin. And this experience of the whole inner man pressing against the surface enabled the pupil to receive a new insight. He was able to say to himself : You have now a feeling and experience of what you would be if, of all the things in the Cosmos, the Sun alone worked upon you. In this way he learned to recognise the working of the Sun in the Cosmos, and how its working is distributed in the Cosmos. He learned to know man's relation to the Sun. And he learned that the reason why man is not in reality what he now felt himself to be under the suggestive influence of the Sun-statue, is because other forces, working in from other corners of the Cosmos, 'mummify' this working of the Sun. In such manner did the pupil learn to find his bearings in the Cosmos, to be, as it were, at home in the Cosmos.

And when the pupil felt the suggestive influence of the Moon-statue, when he had in him the hard frost of numbness and experienced a winter landscape within him (in the case of the Sun-statue, he experienced a summer landscape in the spirit), then he felt what he would be like if the Moon influences alone were present.

What does man really know about the world in the present-day ? He knows, let us say, that the chicory flower is blue, that the rose is red, the sky blue, and so forth. But these facts make no violent or overwhelming impression upon him. They merely tell him of what is nearest at hand, of what is in his immediate environment. If man would know the secrets of the Cosmos, then he must become in his whole being a sense-organ,—and, to an intense degree.

Through the suggestive influence of the Sun-statue, the whole of the pupil's being was concentrated in the circulation of the blood. He learned to know himself as a

Sun-being, as he experienced within him this suggestive influence. And he learned to know himself as Moon-being, by experiencing the suggestive influence of the female statue. And then he was able to tell from out of these inner experiences he had received, how Sun and Moon work upon the human being ; even as we to-day can say, from the experience of our eyes, how the rose affects us, or from the experience of our ears can tell the working of the sound of C sharp, and so on.

Thus the pupils of these Mysteries experienced still, even in Post-Atlantean times, how man is placed, as it were, in the Cosmos. It was for them an immediate and direct experience.

Now what I have related to you to-day is but a brief sketch of the sublime experience that came to men in the Mysteries of Hibernia, and continued so to come until the first centuries of the Christian Era. It was a cosmic experience—this Sun-experience and Moon-experience.

In the Mysteries of Ephesus in Asia Minor the pupil had to undergo experiences of quite a different character. Here he experienced in a particularly intense manner, with the whole of his being, that which later found such perfect expression in the opening words of the John-Gospel : ' In the beginning was the Word. And the Word was with God. And a God was the Word.' In Ephesus, the pupil was led, not before two statues, but before one, —the statue that is known as the Artemis (Diana) of Ephesus. Identifying himself—as I said yesterday—with this statue which was fullness of life, which abounded everywhere in life, the pupil lived his way into the Cosmic Ether. With the whole of his inner feeling and experience he raised himself out of mere earthly life, raised himself up into the experience of the Cosmic Ether. And now he was guided, to a new knowledge. First of all, the real nature of human speech was communicated to him. And then from human speech, from the human image, that is, of the Cosmic Logos, from the humanly-imaged Logos, it was shown to the pupil how the Cosmic Word works and weaves creatively throughout the Universe.

61

Once more, I can only describe these things in bare outline. The process was such that the attention of the pupil was especially drawn to what happens when the human being speaks, when he impresses the mark of his word on the outgoing breath. He was led to experience what happens with that which, through his own inner deed, man leads over into life,—to feel how his ' word " looks in the element of air ; and moreover, how two further processes are united with what takes place in the element of air.

Imagine that we have here the expired air, on which are impressed certain words that the human being speaks. Whilst this breath, formed into words, streams outwards from the breast, the rhythmic vibration goes downwards and passes over into the whole watery element that permeates the human organism. Thus at the level of his throat, his speech-organs, man has the air-rhythms when he speaks. But along with his speaking goes a wave-like surging and seething of the whole fluid-body in the human being. The fluid in man, that is below the region of speech, comes into vibration and vibrates in harmony. This is what it really means when we say that our speech is accompanied by feelings. If the watery element in the human being did not vibrate in harmony in this way, man's speech would go forth from him neutrally, indifferently ; he would not be able to permeate what he says with feeling. And upwards in the direction of the head, goes the element of warmth, and accompanying the words that we impress upon the air are upward-streaming waves of warmth, which permeate the head and there make it possible for our words to be accompanied by thought.

Thus, when we speak, we have to do with three things : air, warmth and water. This process, which alone presents a complete picture of what lives and weaves in human speech was taken as the starting-point for the pupil of Ephesus.

It was then made clear to him that that which thus takes place in the human being is a cosmic process made human, and that in a certain far-off time the Earth itself worked in that way ; only it was not then the air element, but the watery element, the fluid element—which I described yesterday as a volatile, fluid albumen—that had this wave-like moving and surging. Like the air in man, in the microcosm, when he speaks on the outgoing breath, so was once the volatile, fluid element, the albumen which surrounded the Earth like an atmosphere. And as to-day the air passes over into the warmth-element, so the albumen went upwards into a kind of air-element, and downwards into a kind of earthly element. And as with us feelings arise in our body through the fluid element, so in the Earth the Earth-formations, the Earth-forces sprang into existence, all the forces that work and seethe within the Earth. And above, in the airy element the cosmic thoughts were born, the soaring cosmic thoughts that work creatively in the earthly substance.

Majestic and powerful was the impression that the human being received at Ephesus, when he was shown how in his own speech lived the microcosmic echo of what had once been macrocosmic. And the pupil of Ephesus, when he spoke, felt an insight come to him through the experience of speech into the working of the Cosmic Word. He could perceive how the Cosmic Word set in motion the volatile fluid element, giving it movement full of meaning and import ; he saw too how it went upward to the creative cosmic thought, and downward to the Earth-forces coming into being.

Thus did the pupil live his way into the Cosmos, by learning to understand aright what was in his own being. ' Within thee is the human Logos. The human Logos works from out of thee during thy time on Earth. Thou, as man, art the human Logos.' (For in very deed through that which streams downwards in the fluid element we are ourselves formed and moulded out of speech, whilst through that which streams upwards, we have our human thoughts during our time on Earth.) ' And even as in thee the essence of humanity is the microcosmic Logos, so once in the far-off beginning of things was the Logos, and It was with God and Itself was a God.'

63

In Ephesus men had a profound understanding of this for they understood it in and through the human being.

In considering such a personality as is concealed behind the name of Gilgamish, you must remember how he led his life in the whole milieu and environment that radiated out from the Mysteries. For all culture, all civilisation, was in earlier times a radiation from the Mysteries ; so that when I name Gilgamish to you, you must think of him—as long as he was living in Erech—not indeed as himself initiated into the Mysteries of Erech, but as living in a civilisation that was permeated with the feeling and experience man could have from his relation to the Cosmos.

An experience then came to this personality during his journey to the West, which made him directly acquainted, not with the Hibernian Mysteries themselves—he did not travel so far afield—but with what was cultivated in a colony of the Hibernian Mysteries, situated, as I told you, where the Burgenland now is. What he experienced there lived in his soul and then developed further in the life between death and new birth ; and in the next earthly life he underwent at Ephesus a deepening of the soul in connection with this same experience.

The deepening of the soul took place for both the individuals of whom we have been speaking. Verily it was as though a torrent surged up from the depth of the civilisation of that time and broke like a great wave on the souls of these two. They experienced in vivid and intense reality what survived in Greece after the Homeric period only as a beautifiul semblance, as the glory of something that is gone.

In Ephesus one could still have a feeling of the whole Reality in which man had once upon a time been living, in the days when he still had an immediate relation to the Divine-Spiritual ; when Asia was for him only the lowest of the heavens, when he still had connection with the higher heavens bordering upon it. In those far-off times man had experienced in ' Asia ' the presence of the Nature Spirits, and above, the presence of the Angels, Archangels, etc., and above them again, the Exusiai and the rest of the Hierarchies. Of all this one could still have as it were an after-feeling in Ephesus, in the place, that is, where Heraclitus also lived and where so much of the old Reality was still experienced even in later Grecian times, down to the 6th and 5th centuries B.C.

It was indeed characteristic of the Greek that he took what had once been experienced by man in connection with the Cosmos and steeped it in the myth, in beauty, in the element of art, turning it into images that man felt more human and more near to him.

Now we must turn our thoughts to a time when on the one hand the Greek civilisation had reached its zenith, when it had proudly pushed back, in the Persian wars, the last thrust as it were of the old Asiatic Reality, a time when however on the other hand Greece itself was already beginning to decline ; and we must picture to ourselves what a man of such a time would experience if he still bore in his soul the unmistakable echoes of what had once been the Divine-Spiritual earthly Reality in body, soul, and spirit of mankind.

We shall have to see how Alexander the Great and Aristotle lived in a world that was not altogether adapted to them, in a world indeed that held great tragedy for them. The fact is, Alexander and Aristotle stood in an altogether different relation to the Spiritual from the men around them ; for although they cannot be said to have concerned themselves very much with the Samothracian Mysteries, they had nevertheless a strong affinity in their souls to what went on with the Kabiri in those Mysteries. And right on into the Middle Ages there were those who understood what this meant. Men of the present day build up altogether false ideas of the Middle Ages : they do not realise that there were individuals of all classes in life, on into the 13th and 14th centuries, who possessed a clear spiritual vision, at any rate in that realm which in the ancient East was designated as ' Asia.' The Song of Alexander that was composed by a certain priest in the early Middle Ages is a very significant document ; in comparison with the account history gives to-day of the doings of Alexander and Aristotle, the poem of the Priest Lamprecht is a sublime and grand conception, still akin to the old understanding of all that had come to pass through Alexander the Great.

Take for instance a passage in the poem where a wonderful description is given after the following style. When Springtime comes, you go out into the woods. You come to the edge of the wood. Flowers are blooming there, and the sun stands where it lets the shadow fall from the trees on to the flowers. And there you may see how in the shadow of the trees in Spring spiritual flower-children come forth from the calices of the flowers and dance in chorus at the edge of the wood.

In this description of Lamprecht the Priest we can perceive distinctly shining through, an old and real experience which was still accessible to men of that time. They did not go out into the woods, saying prosaically : Here is grass, and here are flowers, and here the trees begin ; but when they approached the wood while the sun stood behind it and the shadow fell across the flowers, then in the shadow of the trees there came towards them from the flowers a whole world of flower-beings—beings that were actually present to them before they entered into the wood. For when they came in the wood itself they perceived quite other elemental spirits. This dance of the flower-spirits appeared to Lamprecht the Priest and he delighted especially in picturing it. It is indeed significant, my dear friends ; Lamprecht, even as late as the 12th or beginning of the 13th century wishing to describe the campaigns of Alexander, permeates them everywhere with descriptions of Nature that still contain the manifestations of the elemental kingdoms. Underlying his Song of Alexander, there was this consciousness : ' To describe what took place once upon a time in Macedonia when Alexander began his journeys into Asia, when Alexander was taught by Aristotle, we cannot merely describe the prosaic Earth as the environment of these events ; no, to describe them worthily we must include with the prosaic Earth the kingdoms of the elemental beings.'

How different from a modern book of history, which is, of course, quite justified for present times. There you will read how Alexander, against the counsel of his teacher Aristotle whom he disobeyed, conceived himself to have the mission to reconcile the barbarians with civilised mankind, creating so to speak an average of culture ; the civilised Greeks, the Hellenes, the Macedonians and the barbarians.

That, no doubt, is right enough for modern time. And yet how puerile, compared to the real truth ! On the other hand we have a wonderful impression when we look at the picture Lamprecht gives us of the campaigns of Alexander, attributing to them quite a different goal. We feel as though what I have just described—the entry of the Nature-elemental kingdoms, of the Spiritual into the Physical in Nature,—were intended merely as an introduction. For what is the aim of Alexander's campaigns in the *Alexanderlied* of Lamprecht ?

Alexander comes to the very gates of Paradise. Translated as it is into the Christian language of his time, this corresponds in a high degree, as I shall presently explain, to the real truth. For the campaigns of Alexander were not undertaken for the mere sake of conquest, still less against the advice of Aristotle to reconcile the barbarians with the Greeks. No, they were permeated by a real and lofty spiritual aim. Their impulse came out of the spirit. Let us read of it in Lamprecht's poem, who in his own way with great devotion, albeit 15 centuries after the life of Alexander, tells the heroic story. He tells us how Alexander came up to the gates of Paradise, but could not enter in, for, as Lamprecht says, he alone can enter Paradise who has the true humility, and Alexander, living in pre-Christian time, could not yet have that. Only Christianity could bring to mankind the true humility.

Nevertheless, if we conceive the thing not in a narrow but in a broad-minded way, we shall see how Lamprecht, the Christian priest, still feels something of the tragedy of Alexander's campaigns.

It is not without purpose that I have spoken of this 'Song of Alexander.' For now you will not be surprised if we take our start from the campaigns of Alexander in order to describe what went before and what went after in the history of Western mankind, in its connection with the East. For the real underlying feeling of these things was still widely present, as we have seen, at a comparatively late period in the Middle Ages. Not only so ; it was present in so concrete a form that the 'Song of Alexander' could arise, describing as it does with wonderful dramatic power the events that were enacted through the two souls whom I have characterised.

The significance of this moment in the history of Macedonia reaches on the one hand far back into the past, and on the other hand far on into the future. And it is essential to bear in mind how something of a world-tragedy hangs over all that has to do with Aristotle and Alexander. Even externally the tragedy comes to light. It shows itself in this, my dear friends. Owing to peculiar circumstances— circumstances that were fateful for the history of the world —only the smallest part of the writings of Aristotle have come into Western Europe, and there been further studied and preserved by the Church. In point of fact it is only the writings that deal with logic or are clothed in logical form.

A serious study, however, of the little that is preserved of Aristotle's scientific writings will show what a powerful vision he still had of the connection of the whole Cosmos with the human being. Let me draw your attention to a single passage.

We speak to-day of the earth-element, the water-element, the air-element, the fire- or warmth-element, and then of the Ether. How does Aristotle represent all this ? He shows the Earth, the hard firm Earth ; the fluid Earth, the Water ; then the Air ; and the whole permeated and surrounded with Fire. But for Aristotle the 'Earth' in this sense teaches up as far as the Moon. And from the Cosmos, reaching from the stars to the Moon, not, that is to say, into the Earth-realm, but only as far as the Moon, coming towards us, as it were, from the Zodiac, from the stars—is the Ether, filling cosmic space. The Ether reaches downwards as far as the Moon.

All this may still be read by scholars in the books that have been written about Aristotle. Aristotle himself, however, used continually to say to his pupil Alexander : That Ether that is away there beyond the realm of earthly warmth—the light-ether, the chemical ether and the life-ether—was once upon a time united with the Earth. It came in as far as to the Earth. And when the Moon withdrew in the ancient epoch of evolution, then the Ether withdrew from the Earth. And so all that is around us in space as dead world—so ran Aristotle's teaching to his pupil Alexander—is not permeated by Ether. When however, Springtime approaches, and plants, animals and human beings come forth to new life on the Earth, then the elementary spirits bring down again the Ether from out of the realm of the Moon, bring it down into these new-born beings. Thus is the Moon the shaper and moulder of beings.

Standing before that great female figure in the Hibernian Mysteries, the pupil of the Mysteries had a most vivid experience of how the Ether does not really belong to the Earth, but is brought down thither by the elementary spirits, every year, in so far as it is needed for the upspringing into life.

And this was so for Aristotle. He, too, had a deep insight into the connection of the human being with the Cosmos. His pupil Theophrastus did not let the writings come westwards that treat of these things. Some of them, however, went to the East, where there was still an understanding for such truths. Thence they were brought by Jews and Arabs through North Africa and Spain to the West of Europe, and there met, in a manner that I shall have yet to describe, with the radiation of the Hibernian Mysteries, as these expressed themselves in the civilisation and culture of the peoples.

But now all that I have been describing to you was no more than the starting-point for the teaching that Aristotle gave to Alexander. It was a teaching that belonged entirely to inner experience. I might describe it in outline somewhat as follows. Alexander learned from Aristotle to understand how the earthy, watery, airy and fiery elements that live outside the human being in the world around him live also within the human being himself, and how he is in this connection a true microcosm. He learned how in the bones of the human being lives the earthy element, and how in his circulation and in all the fluids and humours in him lives the watery element. The airy element works in all that has to do with the breathing, and the fiery element lives in the thoughts of man. Alexander had still the conscious knowledge of living in the elements.

And with this experience of living in the elements of the world went also the experience of a near and intimate relationship with the Earth. In these days we travel East, West, North, South, but have no feeling for what streams into our being the while ; we only see what our external senses perceive, we only see what the earthly substances in us, not what the elements in us perceive.

Aristotle, however, was able to teach Alexander : When you go eastwards over the Earth, you pass more and more into an element that dries you up . You pass into the Dry.

You must not imagine this to mean that when one travels to Asia one is completely dried up. We have here, of course, to do with fine and delicate workings, that Alexander was perfectly able to feel in himself after he had received the guidance and instruction of Aristotle. When he was in Macedonia he could feel : I have a certain measure of dampness or moistness in me, that diminishes as I go eastward. In this way, as he wandered over the Earth he felt its configuration, as you may feel a human being by touching him, let us say by drawing your hand caressingly over some part of his body, feeling the difference between nose and eye and mouth. So was a personality such as I have described to you able to perceive a difference between

70

the experience he had when he came more and more into the Dry, and the experience that was his on the other hand in going westward and coming more and more into the Moist.

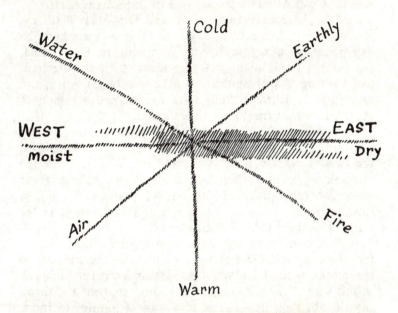

The other differentiations man still experiences to-day, though crudely. In the direction of the North he experiences the Cold ; in the direction of the South the Warm, the Fire element. But the interplay of Moist and Cold, when one goes North-West—that is no longer experienced.

Aristotle awakened in Alexander all that Gilgamish had passed through when he undertook the journey over to the West. And the result of it was that his pupil could perceive in direct inner experience what is felt in the direction of North-West, in the intermediate zone between Moist and Cold :—Water. A man like Alexander not merely could, but did actually speak in such a manner as not to say : There goes the road to the North-West—but instead : There goes the road to where the element of Water holds dominion. In the intermediate zone between Moist and Warm lies the element where the Air holds dominion.

Such was the teaching in the ancient Greek Chthonian Mysteries, and in the ancient Samothracian Mysteries ; and thus did Aristotle teach his own immediate pupil.

And in the zone between Cold and Dry—that it to say, looking from Macedonia, towards Siberia—men had the experience of a region of the Earth where Earth itself, the earthy, holds dominion—the element Earth, the hard and the firm. In the intermediate zone between Warm and Dry, that is, towards India, was experienced a region of the Earth where the Fire element ruled.

And so it was that the pupil of Aristotle pointed North-West and said : There I feel the Water-Spirits working upon the Earth ; pointed South-West and said : There I feel the Air-Spirits ; pointed North-East and there beheld hover especially the Spirits of the Earth ; pointed South-East towards India, and saw the Spirits of Fire hover over the Earth, saw them there in their element.

And in conclusion, my dear friends, you will be able to feel the deep and close relation both to the natural and to the moral, when I tell you how Alexander began to speak in this way : I must leave the Cold-Moist element and throw myself into the Fire—I must undertake a journey to India. That was a manner of speaking that was as closely bound up with the natural as it was with the moral. I shall have more to say about this tomorrow.

I wanted to-day to give you a picture of what was living in those times ; for in all that took place between Alexander and Aristotle we may see at the same time a reflection of the great and mighty change that was taking place in the world's history.. In those days it was still possible to speak in an intimate way to pupils, of the great Mysteries of the past. But then mankind began to receive in increasing measure logic, abstract knowledge, categories, and to push back the other.

We have therefore to see in these events the working of a tremendous and deep change in the historical evolution of mankind, and at the same time an all-important moment in the whole progress of European civilisation in its connection with the East.

V

AMONG THE MYSTERIES OF ANCIENT TIMES Ephesus holds a unique position. You will remember that in considering the part played by Alexander in the evolution of the West, I had to mention also this Mystery of Ephesus. Let us try to see wherein lies the peculiar importance of this Mystery.

We can only grasp the significance of the events of earlier and of more recent times when we understand and appreciate the great change that took place in the character of the Mysteries (which were in reality the source whence all the older civilisations sprang) in passing from the East to the West, and, in the first place, to Greece. This change was of the following nature.

When we look back into the older Mysteries of the East, we have everywhere the impression : The priests of the Mysteries are able, from their own vision, to reveal great and important truths to their pupils. The farther back we go in time, the more are these Wise Men or Priests in a position to call forth in the Mysteries the immediate presence of the Gods themselves, the Spiritual Beings who guide the worlds of the planets, who guide the events and phenomena of Earth. The Gods were actually there present.

The connection of the human being with the macrocosm was revealed in many different Mysteries in an equally sublime manner to that I pictured for you yesterday, in connection with the Mysteries of Hibernia and also with the teachings that Aristotle had still to give to Alexander the Great. An outstanding characteristic of all ancient Oriental Mysteries was that moral impulses were not sharply distinguished from natural impulses. When Aristotle points Alexander to the North-West, where the

75

Spirits of the element of Water held dominion, it was not only a physical impulse that came from that quarter—as we to-day feel how the wind blows from the North-West and so forth—but with the physical came also moral impulses. The physical and the moral were one. This was possible, because through the knowledge that was given in these Mysteries—the Spirit of Nature was actually perceived in the Mysteries—man felt himself one with the whole of Nature. Here we have something in the relation of man to Nature, that was still living and present in the time that intervened between the life of Gilgamish and the life of the individuality Gilgamish became, who was also in close contact with the Mysteries, namely, with the Mystery of Ephesus. There was still alive in men of that time a vision and perception of the connection of the human being with the Spirit of Nature. This connection they perceived in the following way. Through all that the human being learned concerning the working of the elementary spirits in Nature, and the working of the Beings of Intelligence in the planetary processes, he was led to this conclusion : All around me I see displayed on every side the plant-world—the green shoots, the buds and blossoms and then the fruit. I see the annual plants in the meadows and on the country-side, that grow up in Spring-time and fade away again in Autumn. I see, too, the trees that go on growing for hundreds of years, forming a bark on the outside, hardening to wood and reaching downwards far and wide into the Earth with their roots. But all that I see out there —the annual herbs and flowers, the trees that take firm hold into the Earth—once upon a time, I, as man, have borne it all within me.

You know how to-day, when there is carbonic acid in the air, that has come about through the breathing of human beings, we can feel that we ourselves have breathed out the carbonic acid, we have breathed it into space. We have therefore still to-day this slight connection with the Cosmos. Through the airy part of our nature, through the air that gives rise to the breathing and other air-processes that go

76

on in the human organism, we have a living connection with the great Universe, with the Macrocosm. The human being to-day can look upon his out-breathed breath, upon the carbonic acid that was in him and is now outside him. But just as we are able to-day to look upon the carbonic acid we have breathed out—we do not generally do so, but we could—so did the initiates of olden times look upon the whole plant-world. Those who had been initiated in the Oriental Mysteries, or had received the wisdom that streamed forth from the Oriental Mysteries, were able to say : I look back in the evolution of the world to an ancient Sun epoch. In that time I bore still within me the plants. Then afterwards I let them stream forth from me into the far circles of Earth existence. But as long as I bore the plants within me, while I was still that Adam Cadmon who embraced the whole Earth and the plant-world with it, so long was this whole plant-world watery-airy in substance. Then the human being separated off from himself this plant-world. Imagine that you were to become as big as the whole Earth, and then to separate off, to secrete, as it were, inwardly something plant-like in nature, and this plant-like substance were to go through metamorphoses in the watery element—coming to life, fading away, growing up, being changed, taking on different shapes and forms— and you will by this imagination call up again in your soul feelings and experiences that once lived in it. Those who received their education and training in the East at about the time of Gilgamish were able to say to themselves that these things had once been so.

And when they looked abroad upon the meadows and beheld all the growth of green and flowers, then they said : We have separated the plants from ourselves, we have put them forth from us in an earlier stage of our evolution ; and the Earth has received them. The Earth it is that has lent them root, and has given them their woody nature ; the tree-nature in the world of plants comes from the Earth. But the whole plant-nature as such has been cast off, as it were, by the human being, and received by the Earth. In

77

this way man felt an intimate and near relationship with everything of a plant-nature.

With the higher animals the human being did not feel a relationship of this kind. For he knew that he could only work his way rightly and come to his true place on the Earth by overcoming the animal form, by leaving the animals behind him in his evolution. The plants he took with him as far as the Earth ; then gave them over to her that she might receive them into her bosom. For the plants he was upon Earth the Mediator of the Gods, the Mediator between the Gods and the Earth.

Men who had this great experience acquired a feeling that may be put quite simply in a few words. The human being comes hither to the Earth from the World-All. The question of number does not come into consideration ; for, as I said yesterday, they were all and each within the other. That which afterwards becomes the plant-world separates off from man, the Earth receives it and gives it root. The human being felt as though he had folded the Earth about with a garment of plant growth, and as though the Earth were thankful for this enfolding and took from him the watery-airy plant element that he was able, as it were, to breathe on to her.

In entering into this experience men felt themselves intimately associated with the God, with the chief God of Mercury. Through the feeling : We have ourselves brought the plants on to the Earth, men came into a special relation with the God Mercury.

Towards the animals, on the other hand, man had a different feeling. He knew that he could not bring them with him to Earth, he had to cast them off, he had to make himself free from them, otherwise he would not be able to evolve his human form in the right way. He thrust the animals from him ; they were pushed out of the way and had then to go through an evolution on their own account on a lower level than the level of humanity. Thus did the man of olden times—of the Gilgamish time and later— feel himself placed between the animal kingdom and the plant kingdom. In relation to the plant kingdom he was the bearer, who bore the seed to the Earth and fructified the Earth with it, doing this as Mediator for the Gods. In relation to the animal kingdom he felt as though he had pushed it away from him, in order that he might become man without the encumbrance of the animals, who have consequently been stunted and retarded in their development.

The whole animal-worship of Egypt has to do with this perception. The deep fellow-feeling, too, with animals that we find in Asia is connected with it. It was a sublime conception of Nature that man had, feeling his relationship on the one hand with the plant world and on the other hand with the world of animals. In relation to the animal he had a feeling of emancipation. In relation to the plant he felt a near and intimate kinship. The plant world was to him a bit of himself, and he felt a sincere love for the Earth inasmuch as the Earth had received into herself the bit of humanity that gave rise to the plants, had let these take root in her, had even given of her own substance to clothe the trees in bark. There was always a moral element present when man took cognisance of the physical world around him. When he beheld the plants in the meadow, it was not only the natural growth that he perceived. In this growth he perceived and felt a moral relation to man. With the animal man felt again another moral relation : he had fought his way up beyond them.

Thus we find in the Mysteries over in the East a sublime conception of Nature and of Spirit in Nature. Later there were Mysteries in Greece, too, but with a much less real perception of Nature and of Spirit in Nature. The Greek Mysteries are grand and sublime, but they are essentially different from the Oriental Mysteries. It is characteristic of these that they do not tend to make man feel himself on the Earth, but that through them man feels himself a part of the Cosmos, a part of the World-All. In Greece, on the other hand, the character of the Mysteries had changed and the time was come when man began to feel himself united with the Earth. In the East the spiritual world itself was either seen or felt in the Mysteries. It is absolutely true to say that in the ancient Oriental Mysteries the Gods themselves appeared among the priests, who did sacrifice there and made prayers. The Mystery Temples were at the same time the earthly Guest Houses of the Gods, where the Gods bestowed upon men through the priests what they had to give them from the treasures of Heaven. In the Greek Mysteries appeared rather the images of the Gods, the pictures, as it were, the phantoms,—true and genuine, but phantoms none the less ; no longer the Divine Beings, no longer the Realities, but phantoms. And so the Greek had a wholly different experience from the man who belonged to the ancient Oriental culture. The Greek had the feeling : There are indeed Gods, but for man it is only possible to have pictures of these Gods, just as we have in our memory pictures of past experiences, no longer the experiences themselves.

That was the fundamental feeling that took rise in the Greek Mysteries. The Greek felt that he had, as it were, memories of the Cosmos, not the appearance of the Cosmos itself, but pictures ; pictures of the Gods, and not the Gods themselves. Pictures, too, of the events and processes on Saturn, Sun and Moon ; no longer a living connection with what actually took place on Saturn, Sun and Moon, —the kind of living connection the human being has with his own childhood. The men of the Oriental civilisation had this real connection with Sun, Moon and Saturn, they had it from their Mysteries. But the Mysteries of the Greeks had a pictorial or image-character. There appeared in them the shadow-spirits of Divine-Spiritual Reality. And something else went with this as well that was very significant. For there was yet another difference between the Oriental Mysteries and the Greek.

In the Oriental Mysteries, if one wanted to know something of the sublime and tremendous experience that was possible in these Mysteries, one had always to wait until the right *time*. Some experience or other could perhaps only be found by making the appropriate sacrifice, the appropriate supersensible ' experiments ' as it were, in Autumn,—another only in Spring, another again at Midsummer, and another in the depth of Winter. Or again it might be that sacrifices were made to certain Gods at a time determined by a particular constellation of the Moon. At that special time the Gods would appear in the Mysteries, and men would come thither to be present at their manifestations. When the time had gone by one would have to wait, perhaps thirty years, until the opportunity should come again when those Divinities should once more reveal themselves in the Mysteries. All that related to Saturn, for example, could only enter the region of the Mysteries every thirty years ; all that was concerned with the Moon about every eighteen years. And so on. The priests of the Oriental Mysteries were dependent on time, and also on place and on all manner of circumstances for receiving the sublime and tremendous knowledge and vision that came to them. Quite different manifestations were received deep in a mountain cave and high on the mountain top. Or again, the revelations were different, according as one was far inland in Asia or on the coast. Thus a certain dependence on place and time was characteristic of the Mysteries of the East.

In Greece the great and awful Realities had disappeared. Pictures there still were. And the pictures were dependent not on the time of year, on the course of the century, or on place ; but men could have the pictures when they had performed this or that exercise, or had made this or that personal sacrifice. If a man had reached a certain stage of sacrifice and of personal ripeness, then for the very reason that he as a human being had attained thus far, he was able to have view of the shadows of the great world-events and of the great world-Beings.

That is the important change in the nature of the Mysteries that meets us when we pass from the ancient East to Greece. The ancient Oriental Mysteries were subject to the conditions of space and locality, whilst in the Greek Mysteries the human being himself came into consideration and what he brought to the Gods. The God, so to speak, came in his phantom or shadow-picture, when the human being, through the preparations he had undergone, had been made worthy to receive the God in phantom form. In this way the Mysteries of Greece prepared the road for modern humanity.

Now, the Mystery of Ephesus stood midway between the ancient Oriental Mysteries and the Greek Mysteries. It held a unique position. For in Ephesus those who attained to initiation were able still to experience something of the tremendous majestic truths of the ancient East. Their souls were still stirred with a deep inward experience of the connection of the human being with the Macrocosm and with the Divine-Spiritual Beings of the Macrocosm. In Ephesus men could still have sight of the super-earthly, and in no small measure. Self-identification with Artemis, with the Goddess of the Mystery of Ephesus, still brought to man a vivid sense of his relation to the kingdoms of nature. The plant world, so it taught him, is yours ; the Earth has only received it from you. The animal world you have overcome. You have had to leave it behind. You must look back on the animals with the greatest possible compassion, they have had to remain behind on the road, in order that you might become Man. To feel oneself one with the Macrocosm : this was an experience that was still granted to the Initiate of Ephesus, he could still receive it straight from the Realities themselves.

At the same time, the Mysteries of Ephesus were, so to speak, the first to be turned westward. As such, they had already that independence of the seasons, or of the course of years and centuries ; that independence too of place on Earth. In Ephesus the important things were the exercises that the human being went through, making himself ripe, by sacrifice and devotion, to approach the Gods. So that on the one hand, in the content of its Mystery truths, the Mystery of Ephesus harked back to the Ancient East, whilst on the other hand it was already directed to the development of man himself, and was thus adapted to the nature and character of the Greek. It was the very last of the Eastern Mysteries of the Greeks, where the great and ancient truths could still be brought near to men; for in the East generally the Mysteries had already become decadent.

It was in the Mysteries of the West that the ancient truths remained longest. The Mysteries of Hibernia still existed, centuries after the birth of Christianity. These Mysteries of Hibernia are nevertheless doubly secret and occult, for you must know that even in the so-called Akashic Records, it is by no means easy to search into the hidden mysteries of the statues of which I told you yesterday—the Sun Statue and the Moon Statue, the male and the female. To approach the pictures of the Oriental Mysteries and to call them forth out of the astral light is, comparatively speaking, easy for one who is trained in these things. But let anyone approach, or want to approach, the Mysteries of Hibernia in the astral light, and he will at first be dazed and stupefied. He will be beaten back. These Irish, these Hibernian Mysteries will not willingly let themselves be seen in the Akashic pictures, albeit they continued longest in their original purity.

Now you must remember, my dear friends, that the individuality who was in Alexander the Great had come into close contact with the Hibernian Mysteries during the Gilgamish time, when he made his journey westward to the neighbourhood of the modern Burgenland. These Mysteries had lived in him, lived in him after a very ancient manner, for it was in the time when the West resounded still with powerful echoes of the Atlantean age. And now all this experience was carried over into the condition of human existence that runs its course between death and a new birth. Then later the two friends, Eabani and Gilgamish, found themselves together again in life in Ephesus, and there they entered into a deeply conscious experience of what they had experienced formerly during the Gilgamish time more or less unconsciously or sub-consciously, in connection with the Divine-Spiritual worlds.

Their life during this Ephesus time was comparatively peaceful, they were able to digest and ponder what they had received into their souls in more stormy days.

Let me remind you of what it was that passed over into Greece before these two appeared again in the decadence of the Greek epoch and the rise of the Macedonian. The Greece of olden time, the Greece that had spread abroad and embraced Ephesus also within its bounds, and had even penetrated right into Asia Minor, had still in her shadow-pictures the after-echo of the ancient time of the Gods. The connection of man with the spiritual world was still experienced, though in shadows. Greece was however gradually working herself free from the shadows ; we may observe how step by step the Greek civilisation was wresting its way out of what we may call divine civilisation and taking on more and more the character of a purely earthly one.

My dear friends, it is only too true that the very most important things in the history of human evolution are simply passed over in the materialistic external history of to-day. Of extraordinary importance for the understanding of the whole Greek character and culture is this fact : that in the Greek civilisation we find no more than a shadow-picture, a phantom of the old Divine Presence wherein man had contact with the supersensible worlds, for man was already gradually emerging out of this Divinity and learning to make use of his own individual and personal spiritual faculties. Step by step we can see this taking place. In the dramas of Æschylus we may see placed before us in an artistic picture the feeling that yet remained to man of the old time of the Gods. Scarcely however has Sophocles come forward when man begins to tear himself away from this conscious sense of union with Divine-Spiritual existence. And then something else appears that is coupled with a name which from one point of view we cannot over-estimate— but of course there are many points of view to be considered.

In the older Grecian time there was no need to make written history. Why was this ? Because men had the living shadow of everything of importance that had happened in the past. History could be read in what came to view in the Mysteries. There one had the shadow-pictures, the living shadow-pictures. What was there then to write down as history?

But now came the time when the shadow pictures became submerged in the lower world, when human consciousness could no longer perceive them. Then came the impulse to make records. Herodotus, the first prose historian, appeared. And from this time onward, many could be named who followed him, the same impulse working in them all,—to tear mankind away from the Divine-Spiritual and to set him down in the purely earthly. Nevertheless, as long as Greek culture and civilisation lasted, there is a splendour and a light shed abroad over this earth-directed tendency, a light of which we shall hear to-morrow that it did not pass over to Rome nor to the Middle Ages. In Greece, a light was there. Of the shadow-pictures, even the fading shadow-pictures of the evening twilight of Greek civilisation, man still felt that they were divine in their origin.

In the midst of all this, like a haven of refuge where men found clear enlightenment concerning what was present, as it were in fragments, in Greek culture,—in the midst stood Ephesus. Heraclitus received instruction from Ephesus, as did many another great philosopher ; Plato, too, and Pythagoras. Ephesus was the place where the old Oriental wisdom was preserved up to a certain point. And the two souls who dwelt later in Aristotle and Alexander the Great were in Ephesus a little after the time of Heraclitus and were able to receive there of the heritage from the old knowledge of the Oriental Mysteries that the Mystery of Ephesus still retained. Notably the soul of Alexander entered into an intimate union with the very Being of the Mysteries as far as it was living in the Mystery of Ephesus.

And now we come to one of those historical events of which people may think that they are mere chance, but which have their foundations deep down in the inner connections of the evolution of humanity. In order to gain an insight

85

into the significance of this event, let us call to mind the following. We must remember that in the two souls who afterwards became Aristotle and Alexander the Great, there was living in the first place all that they had received in a far-off time in the past and had subsequently elaborated and pondered. And then there was also living in their souls the treasure of untold value that had come to them in Ephesus. We might say that the whole of Asia—in the form that it had assumed in Greece, and in Ephesus in particular—was living in these two, and more especially in the soul of Alexander the Great, that is to say, of him who afterwards became Alexander the Great.

Picture to yourselves the part played by this personality. I described him for you as he was in the Gilgamish time ; and now you must imagine how the knowledge that belonged to the ancient East and to Ephesus, a knowledge which we may also call a " beholding," a " perceiving,"—this knowledge was called up again in the intercourse between Alexander the Great and Aristotle, in a new form. Picture this to yourselves ; and then think what would have happened if Alexander, in his incarnation as Alexander, had come again into contact with the Mystery of Ephesus, bearing with him in his soul the gigantic document of the Mystery of Ephesus, for this majestic document of knowledge lived with extraordinary intensity in the souls of these two. If we can form a idea of this, we can rightly estimate the fact that on the day on which Alexander was born, Herostratus threw the flaming torch into the Sanctuary of Ephesus ; on the very day on which Alexander was born, the Temple of Diana of Ephesus was treacherously burnt to the ground. It was gone, never to return. Its monumental document, with all that belonged to it, was no longer there. It existed only as a historical mission in the soul of Alexander and in his teacher Aristotle.

And now you must bring all this that was alive in the soul of Alexander into connection with what I said yesterday, when I showed you how the mission of Alexander the Great was inspired by an impulse coming from the configuration of the Earth. You will readily understand how that which in the East had been real revelation of the Divine-Spiritual was as it were extinguished with Ephesus. The other Mysteries were at bottom only Mysteries of decadence, where traditions were preserved, though it is true these traditions did still awaken clairvoyant powers in specially gifted natures. The splendour and the glory, the tremendous majesty of the olden time were gone. With Ephesus was finally put out the light that had come over from the East.

You will now be in a position to appreciate the resolve that Alexander made in his soul : to restore to the East what she had lost ; to restore it at least in the form in which it was preserved in Greece, in the phantom or shadow-picture. Hence his idea of making an expedition into Asia, going as far as it was possible to go, in order to bring to the East once more—albeit in the shadow form in which it still existed in the Grecian culture—what she had lost.

And now we see what Alexander the Great is really doing, and doing in a most wonderful way, when he makes this expedition. He is not bent on the conquest of existing cultures, he is not trying to bring Hellenism to the East in any external sense. Wherever he goes, Alexander the Great not only adopts the customs of the land, but is able too to enter right into the minds and hearts of the human beings who are living there, and to think their thoughts. When he comes to Egypt, to Memphis, he is hailed as a saviour and deliverer from the spiritual fetters that have hitherto bound the people. He permeates the kingdom of Persia with a culture and civilisation which the Persians themselves could never have produced. He penetrates as far as India.

He conceives the plan of effecting a balance, a harmony between Hellenic and Oriental civilisations. On every hand he founds academies. The academies founded in Alexandria, in Northern Egypt, are the best known and have had the greatest significance for later times. Of the first importance however is the fact that all over Asia larger and smaller academies were founded, in which the works of Aristotle were preserved and studied for a long time to come. What

Alexander began in this way continued to work for centuries in Asia Minor, repeating itself again and again as it were in feebler echoes. With one mighty stroke Alexander planted the Aristotelian Knowledge of Nature in Asia, even as far as India. His early death prevented his reaching Arabia, though that had been one of his chief aims. He went however as far east as India, and also into Egypt. Everywhere he implanted the spiritual Knowledge of Nature that he had received from Aristotle, establishing it in such a way that it could become fruitful for men. For everywhere he let the people feel it was something that was their own,—not a foreign element, a piece of Hellenism, that was being imposed upon them. Only a nature such as Alexander's, able to fire others with his own enthusiasm, could ever have accomplished what he did. For everywhere others came forward to carry on the work he had begun. In the years that followed, many more scholars went over from Greece. Apart from Edessa it was one academy in particular, that of Gondi-Shapur, which received constant reinforcements from Greece for many centuries to come.

A marvellous feat was thus performed ! The light that had come over from the East,—extinguished in Ephesus by the flaming torch of Herostratus,—this light, or rather its phantom shadow, now shone back again from Greece, and continued so to shine until the dramatic moment when beneath the tyranny of Rome the Schools of the Greek philosophers were ultimately closed. In the 6th century A.D. the last of the Greek philosophers fled away to the academy of Gondi-Shapur.

In all this we see two elements interworking ; one that had gone, so to speak, in advance, and one that had remained behind. The mission of Alexander was founded, more or less unconsciously, upon this fact : the waves of civilisation had advanced in Greece in a Luciferian manner, whilst in Asia they had remained behind in an Ahrimanic manner. In Ephesus was the balance. And Alexander, on the day of whose birth the physical Ephesus had fallen, resolved to found a spiritual Ephesus that should send its Sun-rays far out to

East and West. It was in very truth this purpose that lay at the root of all he undertook : to found a spiritual Ephesus, reaching out across Asia Minor eastward to India, covering also Egyptian Africa and the East of Europe.

It is not really possible to understand the spiritual evolution of Western humanity unless we can see it on this background. For soon after the attempt had been made to spread abroad in the world the ancient and venerated Ephesus, so that what had once been present in Ephesus might now be preserved in Alexandria,—be it only in a faltering hand instead of in large shining letters—soon after this second blooming of the flower of Ephesus, an altogether new power began to assert itself, the power of Rome. Rome, and all the word implies, is a new world, a world that has nothing to do with the shadow-pictures of Greece, and suffers man to keep no more than memories of these olden times. We can study no graver or more important incision in history than this. After the burning of Ephesus, through the instrumentality of Alexander the plan is laid for the founding of a spiritual Ephesus ; and this spiritual Ephesus is then pushed back by the new power that is asserting itself in the West, first as Rome, later under the name of Christianity, and so on. And we only understand the evolution of mankind aright when we say : We, with our way of comprehending things through the intellect, with our way of accomplishing things by means of our will, we with our feelings and moods can look back as far as ancient Rome. Thus far we can look back with full understanding. But we cannot look back to Greece, neither can we look back to the East. There we must look in Imaginations. Spiritual vision is needed there. Yes, we can look South, as we go back along the stream of evolution ; we can look South with the ordinary prosaic understanding, but not East. When we look East, we have to look in Imaginations. We have to see standing in the background the mighty Mystery Temples of primeval post-Atlantean Asia, where the Wise Men, the Priests, made plain to each one of their pupils his connection with the Divine-Spiritual of the

89

Cosmos, and where was to be found a civilisation that could be received from the Mysteries in the Gilgamish time, as I have described to you. We have to see these wonderful Temples scattered over Asia ; and in the foreground Ephesus, preserving still within its Mystery much that had faded away in the other Temples of the East, whilst at the same time it had already itself made the transition and become Greek in character. For in Ephesus, man no longer needed to wait for the constellations of the stars or for the right time of year, nor to wait until he himself had attained a certain age, before he could receive the revelations of the Gods. In Ephesus, if he were ripe for it, he might offer up sacrifices and perform certain exercises that enabled him so to approach the Gods that they drew graciously near to him.

It was in this world that stands before you in this picture that the two personalities of whom we have spoken were trained and prepared, in the time of Heraclitus. And now, in 356 B.C. on the birth-day of Alexander the Great, we behold the flames of fire burst forth from the Temple of Ephesus.

Alexander the Great is born, and finds his teacher Aristotle. And it is as though from out of the ascending flames of Ephesus a mighty voice went forth for those who were able to hear it : Found a spiritual Ephesus far and wide over the Earth, and let the old physical Ephesus stand in men's memory as its centre, as its midmost point.

Thus we have before us this picture of ancient Asia with her Mystery centres, and in the foreground Ephesus and her pupils in the Mysteries. We see Ephesus in flames, and a little later we see the expeditions of Alexander that carried over into the East what Greece had to give for the progress of mankind, so that there came into Asia in picture-form what she had lost in its reality.

Looking across to the East and letting our imagination be fired by the tremendous events that we see taking place, we are able to view in a true light that ancient chapter in man's history,—for it needs to be grasped with the imagination. And then we see gradually rise up in the foreground the

Roman world, the world of the Middle Ages, the world that continues down to our own time.

All other divisions of history into periods—ancient, medieval and modern, or however else they may be designated —give rise to false conceptions. But if you will study deeply and intently the picture that I have here set before you, it will give you a true insight into the hidden workings that run through European history down to the present day.

VI

OF PECULIAR IMPORTANCE for the understanding of the history of the West in its relation to the East is the period that lies between three or four hundred years before, and three or four hundred years after, the Mystery of Golgotha. The real significance of the events we have been considering, events that culminated in the rise of Aristotelianism and in the expeditions of Alexander to Asia, is contained in the fact that they form, as it were, the last Act in that civilisation of the East which was still immersed in the impulses derived from the Mysteries.

A final end was put to the genuine and pure Mystery impulse of the East by the criminal burning of Ephesus. After that we find only traditions of the Mysteries, traditions and shadow-pictures,—the remains, so to speak, that were left over for Europe and especially for Greece, of the old divinely-inspired civilisation. And four hundred years after the Mystery of Golgotha another great event took place, which serves to show what was still left of the ruins— for so we might call them—of the Mysteries.

Let us look at the figure of Julian the Apostate. Julian the Apostate, Emperor of Rome, was initiated, in the 4th century, as far as initiation was then possible, by one of the last of the hierophants of the Eleusinian Mysteries. This means that he entered into an experience of the old Divine secrets of the East, in so far as such an experience could still be gained in the Eleusinian Mysteries.

At the beginning of the period we are considering, stands the burning of Ephesus ; and the day of the burning of Ephesus is also the day on which Alexander the Great was born. At the end of the period, in 363, we have the day of the death—the terrible and significant death—of Julian the

Apostate far away in Asia. Midway between these two days stands the Mystery of Golgotha.

And now let us examine a little this period of time as it appears in the setting of the whole history of human evolution. If we want to look back beyond this period into the earlier evolution of mankind, we have first to bring about a change in our power of vision and perception, a change that is very similar to one of which we hear in another connection. Only we do not often bring the things together in thought.

You will remember how in my book *Theosophy* I had to describe the different worlds that come under consideration for man. I described them as the physical world ; a transition world bordering on it, namely, the Soul-world ; and then the world into which only the highest part of our nature can find entrance, the Spirit-land. Leaving out of account the special qualities of this Spirit-land, through which present-day man passes between death and a new birth, and looking only at its more general qualities and characteristics, we find that we have to give a new orientation to our whole thought and feeling, before we can comprehend the Land of the Spirits. And the remarkable thing is that we have to change and re-orientate our inner life of thought and feeling in just the same way when we want to comprehend what lies beyond the period I have defined. We shall do wrong to imagine that we can understand what came before the burning of Ephesus with the conceptions and ideas that suffice for the world of to-day. We need to form other concepts and other ideas to enable us to look across the years to human beings who still knew that as surely as man is united through breathing with the air outside him, so surely is he in constant union through his soul with the Gods.

Starting then from this world, the world that is a kind of earthly Devachan, earthly Spirit-land,—for the physical world fails us when we want to picture it,—we came into the interim period, lasting from about 356 B.C. to about A.D. 363 And now what follows ? Over in Europe we find the world from out of which present-day humanity is on the point of emerging into something new, even as the humanity of

94

olden times came forth from the Oriental world, passed through the Greek world, and then into the realm of Rome. Setting aside for the moment what went on in the inner places of the Mysteries, we have to see in the civilisation that has grown up through the centuries of the Middle Ages and developed on into our own time, a civilisation that has been formed on the basis of what the human being himself can produce with the help of his own conceptions and ideas. We may see a beginning in this direction in Greece, from the time of Herodotus onward. Herodotus describes the facts of history in an external way, he makes no allusion, or at most very slight allusion, to the spiritual. And others after him go further in the same direction. Nevertheless in Greece we always feel a last breath, as it were, from those shadow-pictures that were there to remind man of the spiritual life. With Rome on the other hand begins the period to which man to-day may still feel himself related, the period that has an altogether new way of thought and feeling, different even from what we have observed in Greece. Only here and there in the Roman world do we find a personality such as Julian the Apostate who feels something like an irresistible longing after the old world, and evinces a certain honesty in getting himself initiated into the Eleusinian Mysteries.

What Julian, however, is able to receive in these Mysteries has no longer the force of knowledge. And what is more, he belongs to a world where men are no longer able to grasp in their soul the traditions from the Mysteries of the East.

Present-day mankind would never have come into being if Asia had not been followed first by Greece and then by Rome. Present-day mankind is built up upon personality, upon the personality of the individual. Eastern mankind was not so built up. The individual of the East felt himself part of a continuous divine process. The Gods had their purposes in Earth evolution. The Gods willed this or that, and this or that came to pass on the Earth below. The Gods worked on the will of men, inspiring them. Those powerful and great personalities in the East of whom I spoke to you—all that they did was inspired from the Gods. Gods willed : men carried it into effect. And the Mysteries were ordered and arranged in olden times to this end,— to bring Divine will and human action into line.

In Ephesus we first find a difference. There the pupils in the Mysteries, as I have told you, had to be watchful for their own condition of ripeness and no longer to observe seasons and times of year. There the first sign of personality makes its appearance. There in earlier incarnations Aristotle and Alexander the Great had received the impulse towards personality.

But now comes a new period. It is in the early dawn of this new period when Julian the Apostate experiences as it were the last longing of man to partake, even in that late age, in the Mysteries of the East. Now the soul of man begins to grow different again from what it was in Greece.

Picture to yourselves once more a man who has received some training in the Ephesian Mysteries. His constitution of soul is not derived from these Mysteries : he owes it to the simple fact that he is living in that age. When to-day a man recollects, when, as we say, he bethinks himself, what can he call to mind ? He can call to mind something that he himself experienced in person during his present life, perhaps something that he experienced 20 or 30 years ago. This inward recollection in thought does not of course go further back than his own personal life. With the man who belonged, for instance, to the Ephesian civil-isation it was otherwise. If he had received, even in a small degree, the training that could be had in Ephesus, then it was so with him that when he bethought himself in recollection, there emerged in his soul, instead of the memories that are limited to personal life, events of pre-earthly existence, events that preceded the Earth period of evolution. He beheld the Moon evolution, the Sun evolution, beholding them in the several kingdoms of Nature. He was able, too, to look within himself, and see the union of man with the Cosmic All ; he saw how man depends on and is linked with the Cosmos. And all this that lived in his soul was true, ' own ' memory, it was the cosmic memory of man.

We may therefore say that we are here dealing with a period when in Ephesus man was able to experience the secrets of the Universe. The human soul had memory of the far-past ages of the Cosmos.

This remembering was preceded in evolution by something else : it was preceded by an actual living within those earlier times. What remained was a looking back. In the time, however, of which the Gilgamish Epic relates, we cannot speak of a *memory* of past ages in the Cosmos, we must speak of a *present experience* of what is past.

After the time of cosmic memory came what I have called the interim time between Alexander and Julian the Apostate. For the moment we will pass by this period. Then follows the age that gave birth to the western civilisation of the Middle Ages and of modern times. Here there is no longer a memory of the cosmic past, still less an experience in the present of the past ; nothing is left but tradition.

1. Memory of the Cosmic Past.
2. Present Experience of the Past.
3. Tradition.

Men can now write down what has happened. History begins. History makes its first appearance in the Roman period. Think, my dear friends, what a tremendous change we have here ! Think how the pupils in the Ephesian Mysteries *lived with* time. They needed no history books. To write down what happened would have been to them laughable. One only needed to ponder and meditate deeply enough, and what had happened would rise up before one from out of the depths of consciousness. Here was no demonstration of psycho-analysis such as a modern doctor might make : the human soul took the greatest delight in fetching up in this way out of a living memory that which had been in the past. In the time that followed, however, mankind as such had forgotten, and the necessity arose of writing down what happened. But all the while that man

97

had to let his ancient power of cosmic memory crumble away, and begin in a clumsy manner to write down the great events of the world,—all this time personal memory, personal recollection was evolving in his inner being. For every age has its own mission, every age its own task.

Here you have the other side of that which I set before you in the very first lectures of this course, when I described the rise of what we designated ' memory in time.' This memory in time, or temporal memory, had, so to say, its cradle in Greece, grew up through the Roman culture into the Middle Ages and on into modern times. In the time of Julian the Apostate the seed was already sown for the civilisation based on personality, as is testified by the fact that Julian the Apostate found it, after all, of no avail to let himself be initiated into the Eleusinian Mysteries.

We have now come to the period when the man of the West, beginning from the 3rd or 4th century after Christ and continuing down to our own time, lives his life on Earth entirely outside the spiritual world, lives in concepts and ideas, in mere abstractions. In Rome the very Gods themselves became abstractions. We have reached a time when mankind has no longer any knowledge of a living connection with the spiritual world. The Earth is no longer Asia, the lowest of the Heavens, the Earth is a world for itself, and the Heavens are far away, dim and darkened for man's view. Now is the time when man evolves personality, under the influence of the Roman culture that is spread abroad over the lands of the West. As we had to speak of a soul-world bordering on the spiritual world, on the land of the Spirits that is above,—so, bordering on this spiritual oriental world is the civilisation of the West ; we may call it a kind of soul-world in time. This is the world that reaches right down to our own day. And now, in our time, although most men are not at all alive to the fact, another stupendous change is again taking place.

Some of you who often listen to my lectures will know that I do not readily call any period a period of transition, for in truth every period is such,—every period marks a transition from what comes earlier to what comes later. The point is that we should recognise for each period the nature of the transition.

What I have said will already have suggested that in this case it is as though, having passed from the Spirit-land into the Soul-world one were to come thence into the physical world. In modern civilisation as it has evolved up till now, we have been able to catch again and again *echoes* of the spiritual. Materialism itself has not been without its echoes of the spirit. True and genuine materialism in all domains has only been with us since the middle of the 19th century, and is still understood by very few in its full significance. It is there, however, with gigantic force, and to-day we are going through a transition to a third world, that is in reality as different from the preceding Roman world as this latter was different from the oriental.

Now there is one period of time that has had to be left out in tracing this evolution : the period between Alexander and Julian. In the middle of this period fell the Mystery of Golgotha. Those to whom the Mystery of Golgotha was brought did not receive it as men who understood the Mysteries, otherwise they would have had quite different ideas of the Christ Who lived in the man Jesus of Nazareth. A few there were, a few contemporaries of the Mystery of Golgotha, who had been initiated in the Mysteries, and these were still able to have such ideas of Him. But by far the greater part of Western humanity had no ideas with which to comprehend spiritually the Mystery of Golgotha. Hence the first way by which the Mystery of Golgotha found place on Earth was the way of external tradition. Only in the very earliest centuries were there those who were able to comprehend spiritually, from their connection with the Mysteries, what took place at the Mystery of Golgotha.

Nor is this all. There is something else, of which I have told you in recent lectures, and we must return to it here. Over in Hibernia, in Ireland, were still the echoes of the ancient Atlantean wisdom. In the Mysteries of Hibernia, of which I have given you a brief description, were two

Statues that worked suggestively on men, making it possible for them to behold the world exactly as the men of ancient Atlantis had seen it. Strictly guarded were these Mysteries of Hibernia, hidden in an atmosphere of intense earnestness. There they stood in the centuries before the Mystery of Golgotha, and there they remained at the time of the Mystery of Golgotha. Over in Asia the Mystery of Golgotha took place ; in Jerusalem the events came to pass that were later made known to men in the Gospels by the way of tradition. But in the moment when the tragedy of the Mystery of Golgotha was being enacted in Palestine, in that very moment it was known and beheld clairvoyantly in the Mysteries of Hibernia. No report was brought by word of mouth, no communication whatever was possible ; but in the Mysteries of Hibernia the event was fulfilled in a symbol, in a picture, at the same time that it was fulfilled in actual fact in Jerusalem. Men came to know of it, not through tradition but by a spiritual path. Whilst in Palestine that most majestic and sublime event was being enacted in concrete physical reality,—over in Hibernia, in the Mysteries, the way had been so prepared through the performance of certain rites that at the very time when the Mystery of Golgotha was fulfilled, a living picture of it was present in the astral light.

The events in human evolution are closely linked together ; there is, as it were, a kind of valley or chasm moving at this time over the world, into which man's old nearness with the Gods gradually disappears.

In the East the ancient vision of the Gods fell into decay after the burning of Ephesus. In Hibernia it remained on until some centuries after Christ, but even there too the time came when it had to depart. Tradition developed in its stead, the Mystery of Golgotha was transmitted by the way of oral tradition ; and we find growing up in the West a civilisation that rests wholly on oral tradition. Later it comes to rely rather on external observation of Nature, on an investigation of Nature with the senses ; but this after all is only what corresponds in the realm of Nature to tradition, written or oral, in the realm of history.

Here then we have the civilisation of personality. And in that civilisation the Mystery of Golgotha, with all that pertains to the spirit, is no longer perceived by man, it is merely handed down as history.

We must place this picture in all clearness before us, the picture of a civilisation from which the spiritual is excluded. It begins from the time that followed Julian the Apostate, and not until towards the end of the 19th century, beginning from the end of the seventies, did there come, as it were, a new call to humanity from the spiritual heights. Then began the age that I have often described as the Age of Michael. To-day I want to characterise it as the age when man, if he wishes to remain at the old materialism—and a great part of mankind does wish so to remain—will inevitably fall into a terrible abyss ; he has absolutely no alternative but to go under and become sub-human, he simply cannot maintain himself on the human level. If man would keep on the human level, he must open his senses to the spiritual revelations that have again been made accessible since the end of the 19th century. That is now an absolute necessity.

For you must know that great spiritual forces were at work in Herostratus. He was, so to speak, the last dagger stretched out by certain spiritual powers from Asia. When he flung the burning torch into the Temple of Ephesus, demonic beings were behind him, holding him as one holds a sword,—or as it might be, a torch ; he was but the sword or torch in their hands. For these demonic beings had determined to let nothing of the Spirit go over into the coming European civilisation ; the spiritual was to be absolutely debarred entry there.

Aristotle and Alexander the Great placed themselves in direct opposition to the working of these beings. For what was it they accomplished in history? Through the expeditions of Alexander, the Nature knowledge of Aristotle was carried over into Asia ; a pure knowledge of Nature was spread abroad. Not in Egypt alone, but all over Asia Alexander founded academies, and in these academies made a home for the ancient wisdom, where the study of it could still continue. Here too, the wise men of Greece were ever and again able to find a refuge. Alexander brought it about that a true understanding of Nature was carried into Asia.

Into Europe it could not find entrance in the same way. Europe could not in all honesty receive it. She wanted only external knowledge, external culture, external civilisation. Therefore did Aristotle's pupil Theophrastus take out of Aristotelianism what the West could accept and bring that over. It was the more logical writings that the West received. But that meant a great deal. For Aristotle's works have a character all their own ; they read differently from the works of other authors, and his more abstract and logical writings are no exception. Do but make the experiment of reading first Plato and then Aristotle with inner concentration and in a meditative spirit, and you will find that each gives you quite a different experience.

When a modern man reads Plato with true spiritual feeling and in an attitude of meditation, after a time he begins to feel as though his head were a littler higher than his physical head actually is, as though he had, so to speak, grown out beyond his physical organism. That is absolutely the experience of anyone who reads Plato, provided he does not read him in an altogether dry manner.

With Aristotle it is different. With Aristotle you never have the feeling that you are coming out of your body. When you read Aristotle after having prepared yourself by meditation, you will find that he works right into the physical man. Your physical man makes a step forward through the reading of Aristotle. His logic works ; it is not a logic that one merely observes and considers, it is a logic that works in the inner being. Aristotle himself is a stage higher than all the pedants who came after him, and who developed logic from him. In a certain sense we may say with truth that Aristotle's works are only rightly comprehended when they are taken as books for meditation. Think what would have happened if the Natural Scientific writings of Aristotle had gone over to the West as they were and come into Middle and Southern Europe. Men would, no doubt, have received a great deal from them, but in a way that did them harm. For the Natural Science that Aristotle was able to pass on to Alexander needed for its comprehension souls that were still touched with the spirit of the Ephesian age, the time that preceded the burning of Ephesus. Such souls could only be found over in Asia or in Egypt ; and it was into these parts that this knowledge of Nature and insight into the Being of Nature were brought, by means of the expeditions of Alexander. Only later in a diluted form did they come over into Europe by many and diverse ways—especially, for example, by way of Spain,—but always in a very diluted or, as we might say, sifted form.

The writings of Aristotle that came over into Europe direct were his writings on logic and philosophy. These lived on, and found fresh life again in medieval scholasticism.

We have therefore these two streams. On the one hand we have always there a stream of wisdom that spreads far and wide, unobtrusively, among simple folk,—the secret source of much of medieval thought and insight. Long ago, through the expeditions of Alexander, it had made its way into Asia, and now it came back again into Europe by diverse channels, through Arabia, for instance, and later on following the path of the returning Crusaders. We find it in every corner of Europe,—inconspicuous, flowing silently in hidden places. To these places came men like Jacob Boehme, Paracelsus and a number more, to receive that which had come thither by many a roundabout path and was preserved in these scattered primitive circles of European life. We have had amongst us in Europe far more folk-wisdom than is generally supposed. The stream continues even now. It has poured its flood of wisdom into reservoirs like Valentine Wiegel or Paracelsus or Jacob Boehme,—and many more, whose names are less known. And sometimes it met there,—as for example, in Basil Valentine—new inpourings that came over later into Europe. In the Cloisters of the Middle Ages lived a true alchemistic wisdom, not an alchemy that demonstrates changes in matter merely, but an alchemy that demonstrates the inner nature of the changes in the human being himself in the Universe. The recognised scholars meanwhile were occupying themselves with the other Aristotle, with a misstated, sifted, 'logicised' Aristotle. This Aristotelian philosophy, however, which the scholiasts and subsequently the scientists studied, brought none the less a blessing to the West. For only in the 19th century, when men could no longer understand Aristotle and simply studied him as if he were a book to be read like any other and not a book whereon to exercise oneself in meditation—only in the 19th century has it come about that men no longer receive anything from Aristotle because he no longer lives and works in them. Until the 19th century Aristotle was a book for the exercise of meditation ; but in the 19th century the whole tendency has been to change what was once exercise, work, active power into abstract knowledge,—to change 'do' and 'can' into 'know.'

Let us look now at the line of development, that leads from Greece through Rome to the West. It will illustrate for us from another angle the great change we are considering. In Greece there was still the confident assurance that insight and understanding proceed from the whole human being. The teacher is the *gymnast*. From out of the whole human being in movement—for the Gods themselves work in the bodily movements of man—something is born that then comes forth and shows itself as human understanding. The gymnast is the teacher.

In Rome the *rhetorician* steps into the place of the gymnast. Already something has been taken away from the human being in his entirety ; nevertheless we have at least still a connection with a deed that is done by the human being in a part of his organism. What movement there is in our whole being when we speak! We speak with our heart and with our lungs, we speak right down to our diaphragm and below it ! We cannot say that speaking lives as intensely in the whole human being as do the movements of the gymnast, but it lives in a great part of him. (As for thoughts, they of course are but an extract of what lives in speech). The rhetorician steps into the place of the gymnast. The gymnast has to do with the whole human being. The rhetorician shuts off the limbs, and has only to do with a part of the human being and with that which is sent up from this part into the head, and there becomes insight and understanding.

The third stage appears only in modern times and that is the stage of the *professor*, who trains nothing but the head of his pupils, who cares for nothing but thoughts. Professors of Eloquence were still appointed in some universities even as late as the 19th century, but these universities had no use for them, because it was no longer the custom to set any store by the art of speaking ; thinking was all that mattered. The rhetorician died out. The doctors and professors, who looked after the least part of the human being, namely his head,—these became the leaders in education.

As long as the genuine Aristotle was still there, it was training, discipline, exercise that men gained from their study of him. The two streams remained side by side. And those of us who are not very young and who shared in the development of thought during the later decades of the 19th century, know well, if we have gone about among the country folk in the way that Paracelsus did, that a last remains of the medieval folk-knowledge, from which Jacob Boehme and Paracelsus drew, was still to be found in Europe even as late as the sixties and seventies of the last century. Moreover, it is also true that within certain orders and in the life of a certain narrow circle a kind of inner discipline in Aristotle was cultivated right up to the last decades of the 19th century. So that it has been possible in recent years still to meet here and there the last ramifications, as it were, of the Aristotelian wisdom that Alexander carried over into Asia and that returned to Europe through Asia Minor, Africa and Spain. It was the same wisdom that had come to new life in such men as Basil

105

Valentine and those who came after him, and from which Jacob Boehme, Paracelsus and countless others had drawn. It was brought back to Europe also by yet another path, namely through the Crusaders. This Aristotelian wisdom lived on, scattered far and wide among the common people. In the later decades of the 19th century, one is thankful to say, the last echoes of the ancient Nature knowledge carried over into Asia by the expeditions of Alexander were still to be heard, even if sadly diminished and scarcely recognisable. In the old alchemy, in the old knowledge of the connections between the forces and substances of Nature that persisted so remarkably among simple country folk, we may discover again its last lingering echoes. To-day they have died away ; to-day they are gone, they are no longer to be heard.

Similarly in these years one could still find isolated individuals who gave evidence of Aristotelian spiritual training ; though to-day they too are gone. And thus what was carried east as well as what was carried west was preserved,—for that which was carried east came back again to the west. And it was possible in the seventies and eighties of the 19th century for one who could do so with new direct spiritual perception, to make contact with what was still living in these last and youngest children of the great events we have been describing.

There is, in truth, a wonderful interworking in all these things. For we can see how the expeditions of Alexander and the teachings of Aristotle had this end in view, to keep unbroken the threads that unite man with the ancient spirituality, to weave them as it were into the material civilisation that was to come, that so they might endure until such time as new spiritual revelations should be given.

From this point of view, we may gain a true understanding of the events of history, for it is often so that seemingly fruitless undertakings are fraught with deep significance for the historical evolution of mankind. It is easy enough to say that the expeditions of Alexander to Asia and to Egypt have been swept away and submerged. It is not so. It is easy to say that Aristotle ceased to be in the 19th century. But he did not. Both streams have lasted up to the very moment when it is possible to begin a renewed life of the Spirit.

I have told you on many occasions how the new life of the Spirit was able to begin at the end of the seventies, and how from the turn of the century onwards, it has been able to grow more and more. It is our task to receive in all its fulness the stream of spiritual life that is poured down to us from the heights.

And so to-day we find ourselves in a period that marks a genuine transition in the spiritual unfolding of man. And if we are not conscious of these wonderful connections and of how deeply the present is linked with the past, then we are in very truth asleep to important events that are taking place in the spiritual life of our time. And numbers of people are fast asleep to-day in regard to the most important events of all. But Anthroposophy is there for that very purpose,—to awaken man from sleep.

You who have come here for this Christmas Meeting,— I believe that all of you have felt an impulse that calls you to awaken. We are nearing the day—as this Meeting goes on, we shall have to pass the actual hour of the anniversary— we are coming to the day when the terrible flames burst forth that destroyed the Goetheanum. Let the world think what it will of the destruction by fire of the Goetheanum, in the evolution of the Anthroposophical movement the event of the fire has a tremendous significance.

We shall not however be able to judge of its full significance until we look beyond it to something more. We behold again the physical flames of fire flaring up on that night, we see the marvellous way in which the fusing metal of the organ-pipes and other metallic parts sent up a glow that caused that wonderful play of colour in the flames. And then we carry our memory over the year that has intervened. But in this memory must live the fact that the physical is Maya, that we have to seek the truth of the burning flames

107

in the spiritual fire that it is ours now to kindle in our hearts and souls. In the midst of the physically burning Goetheanum shall arise for us a spiritually living Goetheanum.

I do not believe, my dear friends, that this can come to pass in the full, world-historic sense unless we can on the one hand look upon the flames mounting up in terrible tongues of fire from the Goetheanum that we have grown to love so dearly, and behold at the same time in the background that other treacherous burning of Ephesus, when Herostratus, guided by demonic powers, flung the flaming brand into the Temple. When we bring these two events together, setting one in the background and one in the foreground of our thought, we shall then have a picture that will perhaps have power to write deeply enough in our hearts what we have lost and what we must strive our utmost to build again.

VII

THE LAST GREAT INCISION into the historical evolution of mankind is the one that took place—we have often spoken of it—in the first third of the 15th century, and that marks the transition from the evolution more particularly of the Intellectual or Mind-Soul to that of the Consciousness or Spiritual Soul. For we live in an age when the evolution of the Spiritual Soul is taking place, and it is an age that is entirely bereft of true insight into the connections of the human being with the deeper impulses and forces of Nature, or rather of the Spirit that is in Nature. To-day, when we speak of man and his constitution as physical man, we speak, for instance, of the chemical substances, enumerating them under the heading of what the chemist calls the elements. But it is of about as much value for a man to know that something he eats contains carbon and nitrogen as it is for a watch-mechanic to know that the watch he has in his hand consists of glass and, shall we say, silver and some other substances. All this kind of knowledge that traces back the real substance of man's nature to these material abstractions—hydrogen, oxygen and the like—affords no true knowledge of the human being. The mechanism of the watch has to be understood by seeing in it a connected system of forces ; and similarly, if we would understand the nature and being of man, we must recognise how the various impulses that are to be found working in all the kingdoms of Nature work in the human being ;—for there they work differently than in the other kingdoms of Nature. In modern times however there is no longer any true vision of the connection of man with the Universe. Until the 14th or 15th century this vision and knowledge persisted ;

though degenerate, it was still present in greater or less degree, and instinctively gifted natures were able still to make use of it. But later on, save for a few men like Paracelsus, Jacob Boehme and others, the true insight into man's connection with the Universe, little by little, died completely away.

What does the newer Natural Science, that has gradually grown up since the 15th century, know of the relation, let us say, of the plant world or of the animal world to the human being? The scientist examines the plants in their chemical constitution and tries by some means or other to study these same chemical constituents of the plant as they appear in man. Finally perhaps he tries to form an idea—generally he fails!—of the influence of the substances on the healthy and on the diseased human being. All this investigation however results in a darkening of knowledge. The important thing to-day, if we are really desirous of going forward in our knowledge of man on the foundation of historical insight, is that we should learn to know again what is the real relation of the human being to the Nature that he finds around him.

Until the time of the last great revolution in men's consciousness that took place in the 15th century, there was still a clear perception of the great difference that exists in the metals, as between those that are found in the human being and those that are found in Nature. When we set out to consider the various substances in man's physical nature, certain metals show themselves in greater or less degree. For example, iron is present in the human organism, in combination with various other substances; magnesium is also present, and we could name many others. Before the 15th century men were keenly alive to the difference between such metals as these we have mentioned, that are found when we examine the human organism, and such metals as are present in external Nature but are not at any rate quickly apparent in the human organism. The men of these earlier times said : Man is a microcosm ; whatever is present in the world outside him, in the macrocosm, is present in some form or other in him. And this was for them no mere general principle in the abstract : had they gone but a little way in initiation knowledge, it followed inevitably from what they knew of the nature of man and of the nature of the Universe. They knew that we can only come to a true understanding of man when we bring together in one the whole of Nature, with all her impulses, with all the substances that she contains. Then we have a picture, an imagination of the being of man. And a disturbing element enters the picture when we meet with something outside in Nature that cannot be found in man.

So thought a student of Nature of the 9th, 10th or 11th century. In those times, however, something else was known, namely, that that which man receives by way of physical nourishment is only a part, perhaps not even the most important part, of all that serves to maintain his physical organism, or rather his whole human organism throughout.

Now, to go beyond physical nourishment and include also breathing presents no difficulty to the man of the present day ; for breathing too is a form of assimilation. But it would not occur to him to go any farther. The earlier student of Nature went farther. It was clear to him that when man uses his eye to perceive things, he does not merely see with the eye, but during the process of perception he receives through the eye in infinitely minute quantities something of the substance of the World-All. And not through the eye alone, but through the ear and through other portions of the organism. And the medieval student of Nature was fully aware of the very great importance of those substances which occur in a slight measure only in the human organism, such as, for example, lead, and which man receives in infinitely minute quantities that may be found where we little suspect their presence.

Lead is a metal that cannot immediately be demonstrated as occurring in man. But lead is, as a matter of fact, distributed throughout the entire physical Cosmos in a state of very fine dilution, and the human being takes up lead from the Cosmos by means of processes that are many times more delicate than the process of breathing. The human being is perpetually excreting substances, throwing them off from the periphery. You not only cut your nails, you continually throw off substances from your skin. But whilst substance is thus given off, other substance is taken up and received into the organism.

This was the kind of thought in which a student of Nature lived, who belonged to medieval times,—to the 9th, 10th, 11th or 12th century. He had no balances, he had none of the coarser measuring instruments with which to determine how the substances and forces worked ; for him it was a matter of entering deeply into the inner qualities of Nature, of understanding her inner impulses and her connection with the human being. And men were able in this way to know many things that they will one day begin to know again. For, if truth be told, nothing is known to-day of the real nature of the human being.

You know how when we investigate the constitution of man, we sum it up in the following way,—in order to have some kind of classification and plan : man is composed of physical body, etheric body, astral body and ego, or ego-organisation. Well and good. In the first instance these terms are mere words : but it is good to begin with them, each person can form from them some small idea of the truth. But if we want to make use of this classification in practical life, especially if we want to use it in medicine— admittedly a highly important ' practice ' in life, and one that depends at every step on our knowledge of the human being,—then we cannot possibly remain at the words, we must enter into that which is behind the words and gives them their content. We ask first : what about the physical body ? How can we gain a true idea of it ? (You will see presently why I am developing this line of thought). Take any object on the Earth, outside the human being ; let us say, for instance, a stone. A stone falls to the ground. We say, the stone is heavy, it is attracted by the Earth, it has weight. We discover other forces working in the stone.

If it is formed into a crystal, then form-building forces work in it. These too are related to the earthly forces. In short, when we look around in the world, we find all about us substances that are subject to the earthly nature.

Keep that clearly in mind : we have, to begin with, substances that are subject to the earthly nature.

Someone whose thoughts on these things are not clear, will perhaps come and show you a piece of coal, a piece of black coal. What is it in reality ? In the neighbourhood of the Earth, it is coal ; but the moment you were to take it but a short distance—comparatively speaking—away from the Earth, it would cease to be coal. What makes it coal is nothing but the forces of the Earth. Thus you can say : Here is the Earth, and the forces of the Earth are within it ; but the forces of the Earth are also in every single object that I find here on the Earth. And the physical body of man, although of course it is marvellously combined and held together, is nevertheless essentially such an object, standing in subjection to these physical forces of the Earth, the forces that come from the centre of the Earth. The physical body of the human being can therefore be described as that which is subject to the forces coming from the centre of the Earth.

Now there are other forces on the Earth besides. These other forces come from the whole environment of the Earth, from the far circumference. Imagine for a moment that you are going out and out, away from the Earth into unmeasured distances. From these unmeasured distances forces work upon the Earth, working inwards to it from every direction. Yes, it is a fact, such forces do exist, coming from all directions of the Universe and working in everywhere towards the centre of the Earth. It is possible to gain quite a clear and concrete picture of them in the following way.

You will remember that the most important substance that forms the basis everywhere of the organism, whether it be of plant, animal or man, is albumen. And albumen also forms the basis for the germ of a new plant, animal or human organism. From a fructified germ cell proceeds that which evolves into an organism, and the substance of the germ is albumen. In these days, instead of pursuing true science, men build up all kinds of imaginations, and they make a picture to themselves of this albumen as composed of substances in intricate chemical combination. It is composed, so they say, of carbon, oxygen, hydrogen, nitrogen, sulphur, and a trace too of phosphorus, all in complicate combination. And so the atomist comes to see in albumen the example *par excellence* of chemical combination. The atoms and molecules have to be thought of as arranged in a most complicated manner. And in the mother-animal or mother-plant arises this complicated albumen-molecule, or whatever you choose to call it ; it develops further and the new animal comes to birth from it, arising, that is, purely through inheritance.

From the spiritual point of view, all this is sheer nonsense. The truth is that the albumen of the mother animal is not a complicated chemical combination at all, it is all broken up, destroyed and reduced to chaos. The albumen that is otherwise contained in the body is still to some extent organised, but albumen that forms the basis for propagation is distinguished by this very characteristic, that it is in a condition of complete disorganisation. The substances that are contained in it are reduced to chaos and are in no sort of combination, they are tossed and jumbled together to form a mere accumulation without order or proportion ; and on this very account the albumen is no longer subject to the Earth. So long as the albumen can by some means or other be held together in inward cohesion, so long is it subject to the forces that work from the centre of the Earth. The moment the albumen is inwardly split up and destroyed, it comes under the influence of the whole sphere of the Cosmos. Forces work in upon it from every quarter. And then we have the tiny particle of albumen that forms the basis for reproduction. This tiny particle is an image of the entire Cosmos, because albumen substance has been split up, destroyed and reduced to chaos—converted, that is, into cosmic dust and thereby fitted to become exposed to the working of the entire Cosmos.

Of all this men have to-day simply no knowledge at all. They imagine the old hen has the complicated albumen. This is included in the egg, and thence arises the new hen. It is the albumen continued, it has gone on evolving. Then the germinal substance is developed once again ; and so it goes on from hen to hen. In actual fact it is not so. Every time the transition takes place from one generation to the next, the albumen is exposed to the whole Cosmos.

On the one hand, therefore we have the earthly substances, subject to the earthly or central forces. But we can also imagine these earthly sub-stances exposed in certain circumstances to the forces that work in from all quarters, from the farthest limits of the universe. The latter forces are the ones that work in the human etheric body. The etheric body is subject to the forces of the Cosmos. These are real conceptions of physical body and etheric body.

Suppose you stand there and ask, what is my physical body ? The answer is, it is that body which is subject to the forces proceeding from the centre of the Earth. What is my etheric body ? It is that in you which is subject to the forces streaming in on all sides from the periphery. You can even show it in a drawing. Imagine that this is the human being. His physical body is the one that is subject to the forces that go towards the centre of the Earth. His etheric body is the one that is subject to the forces streaming in from all sides, from the ends of the Universe. Here we have a system of forces in man. There are forces that pull downward,—they are really present in all organs that are upright,—and there are forces that pour in from without, tending inward. You can actually perceive in the form of man where the one kind and the other are more represented. Study the legs and it is obvious, their form is due to the fact that they are more adapted to the earthly forces. The head is more adapted to the forces of the periphery. In like manner you may also study the arms, and this is not uninteresting. Hold your arms close to your body, and they are subject to the forces that go towards the centre of the Earth. Move them in a living way, and you yourself will be subjecting them to the forces streaming in from all sides of the periphery.

Such indeed is the difference between arms and legs. The legs are invariably subject to the central forces of the Earth, while the arms are so only in a certain posture, that is to say, conditionally. Man is able to lift them out of the domain of the earthly central forces and place them in the midst of those forces which we call the ethereal forces, the forces pouring in from the periphery. And so you can see for all the single organs, how they are placed in the whole cosmic system. Here then you have your physical body and your etheric body.

How is it with the astral body? In space, there is no other kind of forces besides these two. The astral body receives its forces from beyond space. While the etheric body receives them from everywhere, from the periphery, the astral body receives them from beyond all space.

We can actually find certain places in Nature where the physical forces of the Earth enter into the midst of the etheric forces that stream in from all sides. You may imagine albumen to begin with as a substance present in the physical Earth. So long as sulphur, carbon, oxygen, nitrogen and hydrogen are in any way chemically recognisable in it, the albumen is in fact subject to the earthly forces. But the moment it enters the sphere of the reproductive process, it is lifted out of the physical forces. The forces of the circumference of the Universe begin to work upon it in its disorganised condition. New albumen comes into being as an image of the whole Universe.

But you see, sometimes the following situation emerges. The disorganisation, the breaking down of the albumen cannot go far enough. You may have albuminous substance of this kind in connection with some animal for instance. For reproduction to take place, it should be possible for it to be divided, broken down entirely, so that it may submit itself to the forces of the whole Cosmos. But the animal is somehow prevented from delivering, for purposes of reproduction, such albuminous substance as would be able straight-away to submit itself to the whole macrocosm. To be capable of reproduction, albuminous substance must submit itself to the whole macrocosm. But the animal in this case is in some way unable to form albuminous substance capable of reproduction without further assistance. This is how it is with the gall-fly. What then does the gall-fly do ? It lays its egg in some part of a plant. Again and again you may find these galls, in oaks, and in other trees where the gall-fly lays her eggs. In the leaf, for instance, you can see these strange formations. Within each one is the egg of a gall-fly. Why does it happen so ? Why is the egg of a gall-fly laid in an oak leaf, with the result that the oak-apple is formed, holding within it the egg, which is *now* able to develop ? The reason for this is as follows. The plant-leaf contains within it an etheric body, which is adapted to the whole cosmic ether. It comes to the assistance of the egg of the gall-fly. Left alone, the gall-fly's egg is helpless. Hence the gall-fly lays it in a portion of a plant which contains already an etheric body included in the whole system of the cosmic ether. The gall-fly therefore approaches the oak in order to get help in the breaking down of its albumen, so that the world-periphery may be

117

able to work *via* the oak leaf, *via* the oak. Alone, the egg of the gall-fly would be doomed to destruction, for it cannot be broken down, it holds together too strongly.

Here we can gain an insight into a strange working of Nature. But this same working is present in Nature in other places too. Suppose for instance that the animal is not merely incapable of providing germ substance which can expose itself to the cosmic ether for the sake of reproduction ; suppose it is not even able to transform any substances within it into inner means of nourishment, that is, to use them for its own inner nourishment. The example of the bee lies near at hand. The bee cannot eat anything and everything. It can only eat what the plant has already prepared for it. And now observe something very strange and remarkable. The bee goes to the plant, seeks out the honey juice, absorbs it, assimilates it within itself, and then builds up what we admire so, the wonderful 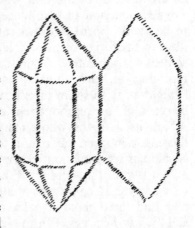 cell structure of the beehive. Here we observe two most strange and wonderful processes : the bee sitting on the flower outside and sucking in the juice, and then, having gone into the beehive, building up from within itself in co-operation with the other bees the cells of wax that will be filled with honey.

What is it that really takes place? You must look carefully at the shape of the cells. They are like this and here comes another joined on to it, and so on, and so on. They are small cells, and similar in form to something else we find in Nature, only there the hollow space is filled up ; they are shaped like quartz crystals, like the crystals of silicic acid. If you go into the mountains and examine the quartz crystals, you will find you can draw them, too, in that form. The drawing will, it is true, show some irregularity of shape, but in the main the form will be similar to the form of the bee-cells that are arranged side by side. Only, the cells of the bee are made of wax and the quartz is made of silicic acid.

When we follow up the matter, we find that long ago at a certain point of time in the evolution of the Earth the quartz-crystal was first formed in the mountains. It was formed under the prevailing etheric and astral influences, with the aid of silicic acid. There you have forces that come from the circumference, working, as ethereal-astral forces, and building the quartz crystals in the silicious substance. Everywhere in the mountains you will find these crystals with their wonderful hexagonal forms. What you find in the solid crystals, you find again as *hollow* forms—as hollow spaces—in the cells of wax, in the beehive.

For what happens ? The bee takes from the flower that which once upon a time brought the quartz crystal into being. The bee fetches it up out of the flower and makes with the substance of her own body imitations of the quartz crystal. A process thus takes place between bee and flower that is similar to what took place long ago in the macrocosm.

I tell you these things that you may understand how necessary it is not merely to take cognisance of the presence of carbon, nitrogen, hydrogen and oxygen, all of which analysis is piteously abstract, but to observe and note the marvellous formative processes, the intimate inner conditions that prevail in Nature and her processes. Once, long ago, science was instinctively built up on such observation. But that all passed away in the course of the historical evolution of mankind ; it came to an end about the 15th century. We must win it back. We must find our way again into the intimate connections of Nature and of her relation with man. Only when we are able once more to recognise such connections can we hope to find again a true insight into the healthy as well as into the diseased human being. Otherwise all pharmacology remains merely a matter of testing and experimenting, without any perception of the inner connections that are at work.

The period from the 15th century until now may be described as an unfruitful period in the evolution of the human spirit. It has borne man down beneath its weight. Man has looked out upon plant and animal, upon human being and upon mineral, and all the while without any real knowledge of them whatsoever ; he has been brought right out of connection with the world and the universe. Now at length it has landed him in chaos as far as his relation with the great world is concerned ; he lives without knowing that he is in any sort of connection with the world around him. In the days when men pondered and meditated upon such things, it was known that every time reproduction took place, the whole macrocosm speaks. In the germ or seed that is capable of reproduction comes to birth a minute image of the whole macrocosm. All around is the great world ; and in the tiniest germ is an offspring of the influences that stream in from the great world from every direction.

In the human being we may see working together, first of all the forces that are the physical-central forces of the Earth. These forces work in all the organs of the human being. But everywhere in him work also, in an opposite direction, the forces that stream in from all sides, the etheric forces. Look at the liver, for example, or the lungs : you will only understand them when you know that in them are working together the forces that come from the centre of the Earth and the forces that come in from every direction from the circumference of the Universe. Then we have also certain organs that are permeated by the astral body, or again by the ego-organisation, whilst others are less permeated by these higher members. In the condition of sleep, of course, the human being as a whole has not his astral body and ego-organisation in him at all. Now imagine that some organ, let us say one of the lungs has through some circumstance become too strongly affected by the forces that stream in everywhere from the Cosmic All. The lung will in consequence become diseased, for a certain harmony and balance is necessary between that which works in the lung from the centre of the Earth and that which streams in upon it from all parts of the circumference. If you can succeed in finding mineral susbtances which will provide a counterpoise in the lung to the too strongly working etheric forces, then you will have a remedy wherewith to eliminate their over-activity. The reverse may also happen. The etheric forces may become too weak, and the physical forces that work from the centre of the Earth grow correspondingly too strong. This time you will search the whole kingdom of the plants to discover something that shall strengthen the etheric forces in the organ where they are weak ; and then you will have your remedy for this condition. It is quite impossible to find even the slightest remedy by an observation of the physical body alone, for the physical body of man has in itself no ground for telling anything about its own constitution. The so-called normal process that goes on in the physical body is a process of Nature. But the process that goes on in illness is likewise a process of Nature. If you have what is called a normal healthy liver, you have a liver in which processes of Nature take place. And if you have a liver in which there is an abscess, you have also a liver in which processes of Nature take place. The difference can never be found by investigating the physical body. All you can do from investigation of the physical body is to establish the fact that the appearance is different in the one case from the other. You can learn nothing of the cause. If you have an abscess on the liver, you will only be able to discover the cause of it when you know that in such a case, for example, the astral body enters much more powerfully into the liver than it should. What you have to do is to drive out of the liver the astral body, which has taken possession there too strongly. From all this it is clear that there is really no possibility of speaking about the healthy and the diseased human being in a way that accords with the facts, unless we go beyond the physical body and include also in our consideration the higher members of man's being. We shall indeed only regain a pharmacology when we go beyond the physical body, for the nature of illness is simply not demonstrable from the physical body alone.

At the present time my purpose is merely to set forth these things in their historical aspect and connections. It must, however, be pointed out that with the gradual dimming and darkening of that which has been brought over from olden times, all real knowledge of the human being has died right away. And now to-day we are faced with the necessity of acquiring once again a knowledge of the human being. Such knowledge will be attainable when we are once again in a position to understand the relationship of the human being to the surrounding kingdoms of Nature.

Suppose, then, we take our start from the ego-organisation of the human being. If, through initiation science, we have attained to imaginative cognition and are able to perceive the ego-organisation of man, then we may ask ourselves : With what portion of the human organism (in its present state) does this ego-organisation stand in especially near relation ? It stands in an especial relation with all that is mineral in the human being. Hence when you receive into yourself some essentially mineral substance,—for example, when you take some salt on your tongue—it is the ego-organisation in you that immediately pounces upon this mineral substance. And as the substance is carried further into the body, all the while,—even when the salt substance is in the stomach—the ego-organisation remains with it. The salt goes still further, it undergoes various changes, it passes through the intestines,—never once does the ego-organisation leave hold of her salt ! They behave like two closely related things, two things that belong to one another : the ego-organisation, and the salt that enters the human being.

It is quite another matter when you eat, for example, a poached egg, or any substance of a similiar—albuminous—consistency. The ego-organisation is very little concerned when you have a piece of poached egg on your tongue. Afterwards, as it slips down into the stomach, the astral body concerns itself with it, but again only to a very small extent. Then it goes further. And now, first the etheric and then the physical body begin to act intensively upon it. They break down within you the albumen that you receive into your organism with the egg. The egg itself is now made entirely of mineral within you. It is broken down and destroyed. All life is driven out of it. It is destroyed within you. At the walls of the intestines the albumen substance that you have taken into you from outside ceases to be albumen in any sense, becomes entirely mineral in character. And now it passes over into the ego-organisation; from this point the mineralised albumen is taken up by the ego-organisation.

Thus, the ego-organisation concerns itself only with what is mineral. And all mineral substances are changed through its action ; in the human organism they become different from what they were outside it. No mineral substance can remain the same within the human organism as it is outside. The ego-organisation has to look after this in a very thorough manner. Nor is it only such substances as cooking salt and the like that are seized upon by the ego-organisation and inwardly changed to something quite different. The human being is surrounded by a certain condition of warmth, but that external condition of warmth must never be allowed to penetrate the human being. You can never have your finger full of that which is all around you as external warmth. This warmth can but act as a stimulus, you yourself must create and produce the warmth that you have within you. The moment you are merely, so to say, an object and do not yourself create your own warmth or cold, but let the warmth from outside extend its influence into you exactly as it does into any external object,—in that moment you become ill. The external warmth,—not even a substance, but the warmth itself makes you ill. Suppose you have here a towel or a sponge, and over there is a fire. The warmth of the fire, which can spread out all around quite easily, will permeate the towel or the sponge. The towel or sponge only carries a little further the radiating warmth of the fire. When, however, the warmth of the fire reaches the skin of the human being and acts upon the senses, stimulating them, then it must no longer simply spread in this way ; then the reaction must come, the inner warmth must be created from within. If a person catches cold, his condition results from the fact that he has not merely let himself be stimulated to create his own inner warmth, but has let the external cold enter to some extent beneath the skin. Thus he does not take his place in the world as a fully active human being who fills himself with his own activity and his own impulses, but plays rather the part of an object that lets the activities and influences of the outer world pass through him. That is the essential nature of the ego-organisation that it takes up into itself what is mineral and completely changes it from within, converting it into something altogether different.

Not until we have died does the mineral turn back again into the mineral of external Nature. So long as we are alive on the Earth, and have the mineral enclosed in our skin, so long does the ego-organisation continue to change it perpetually. Similarly, whatever we take up into ourselves that is of a plant nature is perpetually changed by the working of the astral body. It is in everything of a mineral nature that the ego-organisation brings about a thorough metamorphosis ; not merely in the solid mineral, but also in the liquid and gaseous mineral, and the mineral that is in the state of warmth or heat.

Of course, when we speak in quite an ordinary way, we may say : Here is some water. I drink it. Now I have the water inside me. The truth is, however, that the moment my organism receives the water, then by reason of the action of my ego-organisation, the water inside me is no longer the same as the water outside. It only becomes the same again when I give it off in the form of perspiration, or in some other way convert it into water. Inside my skin water is not water, it is living fluid.

In this manner we shall have to alter our thought about a great many things. To-day I have only been able to give you small indications. Think them over. Think how the albumen has to be broken down and disorganised in order

124

that it may be exposed to the influences of the whole macrocosm. Think how the water I drink becomes in me living fluid and is no longer the inorganic water it was before, but is water permeated by the ego-organisation. Think how, when you eat cabbage—outside you it was cabbage, inside you the astral body receives the cabbage into itself and transforms it into something new. And here we come to the consideration of very important processes in the human body. We learn to perceive how we have in our metabolic system processes that are only one evolutionary stage removed from the metabolisms that we have, for example, in our brain—the metabolisms that go to make up the nervous system, and so forth. I will speak further on this to-morrow and make clear, in connection with these processes, the radical difference between men of the 12th and of the 20th century. We shall thus come to see the necessity for new impulses to enter in, if there is to be progress in the understanding of health and disease, and if the knowledge of man is not to die out altogether and nothing more ever be known of the healthy or of the diseased human being.

VIII

WE STAND TO-DAY UNDER the sign of a painful memory, and I want to place what we have to take for the theme of our lecture to-day into the sign of that painful memory. The lecture I was able to give exactly a year ago in our old Goetheanum,—those of you who were present will remember how it took its start from descriptions of Nature, of relationships that can be observed in Nature on Earth, and led from these up to the spiritual worlds and the revelations of the spiritual worlds in the writing of the stars. And you will remember how we were able then to bring the human heart, the human soul and spirit in their whole nature and being into close connection with what is found when one follows the path that leads away from the earthly into the distant stellar spaces, wherein the spiritual writes its Cosmic Script. And the words that I then wrote upon the blackboard, writing for the last time in the room that was so soon to be taken from us, bore within them this impulse and this purpose : to lift the human soul into spiritual heights.

So on that evening we were brought into direct and close touch with that to which our Goetheanum in its whole intention and character was devoted. And to-day you will allow me to speak to you again of these things, as it were in continuation of the lecture that was given here a year ago.

In the days preceding the burning of Ephesus, when men spoke of the Mysteries, provided they were men who had some understanding and feeling for them, they spoke of them somewhat in the following manner : Human knowledge, human wisdom has a home and a dwelling place in the Mysteries. And when in those olden times the Spiritual Guides of the Universe spoke of the Mysteries, when the

127

Mysteries were spoken of in the supersensible worlds—I may be permitted this expression, although of course it is only a figure of speech to describe how thought and influence streamed down from the supersensible into the sensible worlds—when, therefore, the Mysteries were spoken of in the supersensible worlds, then it was somewhat in the following way : ' In the Mysteries men erect places where we Gods can find the men who do sacrifice and who understand us in the sacrifice.'

For in point of fact men of the old world, men of the old world who knew, were conscious that in the places of the Mysteries Gods meet with men ; they knew how all that carries and sustains the world depends on what takes place between Gods and men in the sacred Mysteries.

But there is a *word*,—a word that has come down to us in history and that can speak powerfully to the human heart even in external historical tradition, but that speaks with peculiar force and earnestness when we see it shape itself out of strange and unparalleled events, when we see it written with eternal letters into the history of mankind, though the writing be only visible for a moment in the spirit. I declare to you that, wherever the eye of the spirit is turned to the deed of Herostratus, to the burning of Ephesus, then, in those flames of fire may be read the ancient word : The Jealousy of the Gods.

Among the many and diverse words that have come down to us from olden time, and that were in use in the life of olden times in the manner I have described,—among all the words in this physical world, this word is, I verily believe, one of the most awful : The Jealousy of the Gods. In those times the term God was applied to all beings of a supersensible nature,—to every form of being that had no need to appear on Earth in a physical body. Many and varied kinds of Gods were differentiated. The Divine-Spiritual Beings who are most closely united with mankind, from Whom man in his innermost nature originated and by Whom he was launched into the stream of time, the same Beings Whom we recognise in the majesty of Nature and in her

128

smallest manifestations, and Whom we discover too in that which lives in our own inmost selves,—these Divine-Spiritual Beings can never be jealous. Nevertheless in that ancient time the ' Jealousy of the Gods ' was something very real to man. If we study the period of human development that led up to the time of Ephesus, we find that the more advanced members of the human race received into their being much of what the good Gods held out to them in the Mysteries. For it is true to say that an intimate relationship exists between good human hearts and the good Gods. and this intimate relationship was knit closer and closer in the Mysteries. And thus it came to pass that certain other divine Beings, Luciferic-Ahrimanic divine Beings were made aware, that man was being drawn nearer and nearer to the good Gods. And there arose a jealousy on the part of the Gods, a jealousy concerning man. Over and over again in human history we have to hear how a man who strives after the Spirit falls victim to a tragic destiny. In olden times such an event was spoken of as brought about by the Jealousy of the Gods.

The Greeks knew very well that this Jealousy of the Gods exists ; they traced back to it much of what took place in the history of man. With the burning of Ephesus it was made manifest that further spiritual evolution was only possible if men became conscious that there are Gods—that is, super-sensible Beings—who are jealous of the further advance of man.

It is this that gives the peculiar colouring to all history that follows the burning of Ephesus,—or I may also say, the birth of Alexander. And it is essential for a right under-standing of the Mystery of Golgotha. We have to see a world filled with the jealousy of certain kinds of Gods. Ever since a time that follows soon after the Persian War, the soul-atmosphere of the world was filled with the effects of this Jealousy of the Gods. And that which had to be done in the Macedonian time had to be done in the full consciousness that the Jealousy of the Gods pervades the spiritual atmosphere over the surface of the Earth. But it was done with courage and daring, and in spite of the misunderstandings of Gods and men.

Into this atmosphere, filled with the Jealousy of the Gods, sank then the Deed of Him Who was capable of the greatest Love that can exist in the world. We only see the Mystery of Golgotha in a true light, when we add to all else we have learned concerning it this picture : the dark bank of cloud that hung in olden time over Greece, Macedonia, Asia Minor, Northern Africa and Southern Europe, the dark cloud that is the expression of the Jealousy of the Gods. And then into this cloud-filled atmosphere we behold streaming down the warm and gentle rays of the Love that pours through the Mystery of Golgotha.

But when we come to our own time, then that which in earlier ages was—if I may put it so—an affair between Gods and men, must in this epoch of human freedom be played out below in the physical life of men. We can already describe how it is being so played out. In olden times, when men thought of the Mysteries, it was in this sense that they spoke of them :—In the Mysteries, they said, human knowledge, human wisdom has a home. And when the Mysteries were spoken of among the Gods, it was said : When we descend into the Mysteries, we find the sacrifice done by human beings, and in the sacrificing human being we are understood. The burning of Ephesus marks the beginning of the epoch that saw the gradual and complete disappearance of the Mysteries in their ancient form.

I have told you how the Mysteries were continued here and there—in a sublime manner, for example, in the Mysteries of Hibernia, where the Mystery of Golgotha was celebrated in the ritual at the very time when it was taking place physically over in Palestine. Men had knowledge of it not through physical but through spiritual means of communication. Notwithstanding these survivals, the real being of the Mysteries retreated more and more in the physical world. The external centres which were the meeting places for Gods and men lost more and more of their significance. By the time of the 13th and 14th centuries it had almost entirely gone.   For whoever would find the way, for example, to the Holy Graal, must know how to tread *spiritual paths*.   In the olden times, before the burning of Ephesus, man trod *physical paths*.   In the Middle Ages it is spiritual paths that he must tread.

Spiritual paths above all were necessary from the 13th, 14th and especially the 15th century onwards, if one wanted to receive true Rosicrucian instruction.   For the temples of the Rosicrucians were hidden from outer physical experience. Many a true Rosicrucian frequented these temples, it is true, but no outer physical eye of man could find them.   None the less there were disciples who came to these old Rosicrucians ; for in scattered places the true Rosicrucians could indeed be found.   They were like hermits of wisdom and of consecrated human action.   And any man who was able to perceive the language of the Gods in the gentle radiance of their eyes, would find them so.   I am not speaking in mere pictures.   I am relating a reality, and a reality which was of cardinal importance for that time. To find the Rosicrucian master the pupil must first attain the faculty to perceive the language of Heaven in the gentle light of the physical eye.   Then it was possible to find here and there in Mid-Europe, in the 14th and 15th centuries, these remarkable men, living in the most simple and unpretentious manner—men who were God-inspired, connected in their inner life with the spiritual temples which did indeed exist, albeit the access to them was no less difficult than the access to the Holy Graal, as described in the well-known legend.

Observing in the spirit what took place between such a Rosicrucian master and his pupil, we can hear many a conversation, wherein is shown once again—though in a form that belongs to a more modern age—how the Wisdom of the Gods lives and moves upon Earth.   For the instructions of these masters were essentially objective and concrete.   There in his loneliness some Rosicrucian master was found by the pupil who had spared no pains to seek him out.   Gazing into the gentle eyes of the master out of which

131

spoke the language of the Gods, this pupil would receive in all humility an instruction somewhat as follows :—

Look, my son, at your own being ! You carry about with you a body which your physical eyes can see. The centre of the Earth supplies this body with the forces which make it visible. This is your physical body.

But look around you at your environment on Earth. Behold the stones! They can exist on Earth by themselves, they are at home here. And if they have once assumed a certain form, they can preserve this form by virtue of the Earthly forces. Look at the crystal ; it bears its form within it. The Earth enables it to keep the form which belongs to its own being. Your physical body cannot do that. When your soul leaves it, it is destroyed, dissolved in dust. The Earth has no power over your physical body. It has the power to form and also to maintain the transparent crystal mountains with their wonderful configuration ; but the Earth has no power to maintain the form of your physical body, it must dissolve it in to dust. Your physical body is not of the Earth, it is of high spirituality. To Seraphim, Cherubim and Thrones belongs the form and figure of your physical body. Not to the Earth, but to the highest spiritual powers which are accessible to men, does this physical body of yours belong. The Earth can destroy it, but never build it up.

And now, within this physical body dwells an etheric body. The day will come when your physical body will be received by the Earth for its destruction. Then will your etheric body dissolve in the wide expanse of the Cosmos. The far spaces of the Cosmos can indeed dissolve, but they again cannot build your etheric body. Only the divine spiritual Beings can build it up—the Beings of the hierarchy of Dynamis, Exusiai and Kyriotetes. To them you owe your etheric body.

With your physical body you unite the physical substances of the Earth. But that which is within you transforms these substances into something utterly different from all that is physically present in the environment of the physical body.

132

Your etheric body brings into movement all that is fluid within you, all that is water within you. The saps and fluids in their circulation stand under the influence of your physical body. Behold your blood ! It is the Exusiai, Dynamis and Kyriotetes who cause the blood to circulate as a fluid through your veins. It is only as a physical body that you are man ; in the etheric body you are still animal, albeit an animal that is inspirited by the second Hierarchy.

What I have here gathered up into a very few words was the substance of a prolonged instruction given by that master in the gentle light of whose eyes the pupil discerned the language of Heaven. And then his attention was turned to the third member of the human being, which we call the astral body. And it was made clear to him that this astral body contains the impulse for the breathing—for all that is airy in the human organism, for all that pulsates as air within this body of ours. Now it is true that for a long time after man has passed through the gate of Death, the earthly nature strives as it were to make disturbances in the airy element, so much so that the clairvoyant vision can observe in the atmospheric phenomena of the Earth for many years, the noising of the astral bodies of the dead. Nevertheless the Earth with its encircling sphere can do no other in relation to the impulses of the astral body too than dissolve them. For these again can only be created by Beings of the third Hierarchy—the Archai, Archangeloi and Angeloi.

And then the master said,—and his words struck deep into the heart of his pupil : In your physical body, inasmuch as you receive within you the mineral kingdom and transform it, you belong to the Seraphim, Cherubim and Thrones. In so far as you are an etheric body, you are like an animal. Here however you belong to the Spirits whom we designated as those of the second Hierarchy—the Kyriotetes, Exusiai, Dynamis. Inasmuch as you live and move in the fluid element, you belong not to the Earth but to this Hierarchy. And as you live and move in the airy element, you belong not to the Earth but to the Hierarchy of Archai, Archangeloi and Angeloi.

When the pupil had received this instruction in sufficient measure, he no longer felt that he belonged to the Earth. He felt forces proceeding from his physical, etheric and astral bodies which united him with the Hierarchies. For he felt how, through the mineral world, he is united with the first Hierarchy ; through the water of the earth, with the second Hierarchy ; and through the atmosphere, with the third Hierarchy. And it was plain to him that he is an inhabitant of Earth purely and solely on account of the element of warmth that he bears within him. In this way the Rosicrucian pupil came to the perception that the warmth, the physical warmth he has within him, is what makes him ' man on earth.' And he learned increasingly to feel how closely related warmth of soul and warmth of spirit are to physical warmth.

The man of later times gradually lost all knowledge of how his physical, etheric and astral content are connected— through the solid, the fluid and the aeriform—with the Divine. The Rosicrucian pupil however knew this well ; he knew that what made him earthly was not these elements at all, but the element of warmth.

The moment the pupil of the Rosicrucian teacher perceived this secret of the connection of the element of warmth with his life on earth as earthly man, in that moment he knew how to link the human in him on to the spiritual.

Now the pupils who came to these oftentime humble haunts where such Rosicrucian masters lived were prepared before-hand in a way that was frequently quite unsought by them and that appeared no less than marvellous in their eyes. An intimation would come to them, to one in one way, to another in another ; often to all outward appearance it came by a mere chance. The intimation would be given to them : You must seek out a place where you may be able to bring your own spiritual nature into contact with the Spiritual of the Cosmos. And after the pupil had received the instruction of which I told you, then, yes then, he was able to say to the master : I go from you with the greatest comfort that could ever be to me on Earth. For in that you have shown to me how earthly man has his own proper element in warmth, you have opened to me the possibility to connect my physical nature with soul and spirit. The hard bones, the flowing blood, the airy breath,— into none of these do I bring my soul nature, but only into the element of warmth.

It was with an infinite peace and rest that the pupils departed from their masters in those days. In their countenance was expressed the great comfort they had received, and from this look of peace developed gradually that mild and gentle gaze whence the language of Heaven can speak. And so we find in those earlier times and on into the first third of the fifteenth century a profound instruction of the soul being given in these humble and secluded haunts. It is indeed unknown as compared with the events of which external history relates. It went on none the less, and was an instruction that took deep hold of the entire human being, an instruction that made it possible for the human soul to link its own nature on to the sphere of the Cosmic-Spiritual.

This whole spiritual atmosphere has disappeared in the course of the later centuries. It is no longer present in our civilisation. An external, God-estranged civilisation has spread abroad over the countries that once upon a time saw such a civilisation as I have just described to you. We stand here to-day bearing within us the memory of many a scene like that I have described, although the memory can only be created in the Spirit in the astral light. And when we look back into the older times, that are so often pictured to us as times of darkness, and then turn our gaze upon our own times, a deep longing arises in our hearts. From out of the spiritual revelations that have been accessible to man since the last third of the nineteenth century, is born a longing to speak to men once more in a spiritual way. But to do so it is not enough to speak with abstract words ; to speak spiritually demands the use of manifold signs and symbols ; our speech has to be wide and comprehensive. Such a language, my dear friends, such a form of speech as needed to be found for the Spiritual Beings Who have to speak to modern humanity, was given to us in the forms of the Goetheanum that was destroyed by fire a year ago. In very truth, the forms were built and moulded to that end, that what was spoken from the platform in ideas should speak on further in them.

And so in a certain sense we may say that in the Goetheanum we had something that could awaken in an altogether new form a memory of the old.

When the pupil for initiation entered the Temple of Ephesus, his attention was directed to the statue of which I have spoken to you in these lectures, and the statue called to him in the language of the heart with these words : Unite yourself with the Cosmic Ether, and you will behold the earthly from out of the Ether heights.

Many a pupil at Ephesus did so behold the earthly from out of the Ether heights. And a certain race of the Gods was jealous. Centuries before the Mystery of Golgotha took place, brave men were already finding a way to meet this Jealousy of the Gods. They found a way to foster what had come down to them from ancient holier years of mankind's history and had worked powerfully in human evolution up to the time of the burning of Ephesus. True, it was dim now and feeble, but even in this enfeebled form it could still continue to work.

Had our Goetheanum been brought to completion, then as you entered from the West, your glance would have fallen on a Statue that bade man know himself in his cosmic nature, know himself as a being set between the powers of Lucifer and Ahriman, God-maintained in the midst in inner balance of being. And when you looked upon the forms of the columns and of the architrave, these forms spoke a language that was a continuation of the language which was spoken in words from the platform, where it was sought to express the spiritual in ideas. The sound of the words flowed on into the plastically moulded forms. And above in the dome were displayed the scenes which could bring before the eye of the soul the past evolution of mankind. Whoever looked upon this Goetheanum with feeling and understanding could find in it a memory of the Temple of Ephesus.

The memory, however, grew to be terribly painful. For in a manner not at all unlike that which befell Ephesus in earlier time, exactly at the moment in its evolution when the Goetheanum was ready to become the bearer of the renewal of spiritual life, in that very moment was flung into it the burning brand.

My dear friends, our pain was deep and indescribable. But we made the resolve to go forward, unhindered by this tragedy that had befallen us, to continue our work for the spiritual world. For we were able to say to ourselves in the depths of our own hearts : When we look upon the flames that rose from Ephesus, we behold written into the flames these words : The Jealousy of the Gods. That was a time when men were still unfree and must needs follow the Will of the good and the evil Gods. In our day men are marked out for freedom. A year ago, on New Year's Eve, we beheld the destroying flames. The red glow rose to Heaven. Tongues of flame, dark blue and reddish yellow, curled their way up through the general sea of fire. They came from the metal instruments concealed in the Goetheanum ; the gigantic sea of fire glowed with all manner of changing colours. And as one gazed into this sea of flame with its swift lines and tongues of colour, one had perforce to read these words, words that spoke pain for the soul : The Jealousy of Man.

Thus are the words that speak from epoch to epoch in human evolution bound together in deepest calamity and unhappiness. In the time when man still looked up to the Gods in unfreedom, but had it as his task to make himself free, there was a word that was significant of the deepest unhappiness and grief to him. He beheld inscribed into the flames : The Jealousy of the Gods. And by a thread of spiritual evolution our own calamity is linked with this word. We live in a time when man has to find in himself the power of freedom, and now we behold inscribed in the flames another word : The Jealousy of Man. In Ephesus the statue of the Gods ; here in the Goetheanum the statue of Man, the statue of the Representative of mankind, Christ Jesus. In Him, identifying ourselves in all humility with Him, we thought to attain to knowledge, even as once in their way, a way that is no longer fully understood by mankind to-day, the pupils of Ephesus attained to knowledge in Diana of Ephesus.

The pain does not grow less when one beholds in the light of history what that New Year's Eve brought to us a year ago. When for the last time it was given to me to stand on the platform that was itself built in harmony with the whole Goetheanum, it was my intention and purpose to direct the gaze, the spiritual gaze of those present away from earthly realms to the ascent into the starry worlds where the Will and Wisdom, where the Light of the Spiritual Cosmos are brought to expression. I know well, sponsors were there present at that time,—spirits of those who in the Middle Ages taught their pupils in the manner I have described to you.

One hour after the last word had been spoken, I was summoned to the fire at the Goetheanum. At the fire of the Goetheanum we passed the whole of that New Year night.

One has but to speak these words, and thoughts unutterable surge up in all our hearts and souls. But whenever it has happened in the evolution of mankind that something sacred to that evolution has been torn away, then there have always been a few who have pledged themselves, after the dissolution of the physical, to continue the work in the Spirit, to which the physical was dedicated. And gathered here as we are in the moment that marks the anniversary of the tragic loss of our Goetheanum, we do well to remember that we shall bring our souls into the right attitude for this gathering when we pledge ourselves one and all to bear onward in the Spirit on the advancing wave of human progress that which was expressed in physical form and in physical image in the Goetheanum, and which has been torn away from physical sight by a deed like the deed of Herostratus. Our pain and grief cling to the old Goetheanum. But we shall only show ourselves worthy of having been permitted to build this Goetheanum, if we fulfil the task that yet remains to us, if we take to-day a solemn pledge, each one of us before the highest, the Divine, that he bears within his soul, a pledge to hold faithfully in remembrance the spiritual impulses that have had their outward expression in the Goetheanum that is gone. The Goetheanum could be taken from us : the spirit of the Goetheanum, if so be that in all sincerity we will to keep it, can never be taken from us. It will least of all be taken from us, if in this solemn hour, that is divided by but a short space of time from the actual moment a year ago, when the flames burst forth from our beloved Goetheanum, —if in this solemn hour we not only feel a renewal of our pain, but out of the very pain pledge ourselves to remain loyal to the Spirit to which we erected our Goetheanum, building it up through ten years of work. If this resolve wells up to-day in all sincerity from the depths of our hearts, if we are able to change the pain and grief into the impulse to action, then we shall also change the sorrowful event into blessing. The pain cannot thereby be made less, but it rests with us to find in the pain the urge to action, to action in the Spirit.

Even so let us look back upon the terrible flames of fire that filled us with such unutterable sadness, but let us at the same time feel how to-day, as we dedicate ourselves with solemn vow to the highest divine forces that are within us, a spiritual flame lights up in our hearts. Yea, and the flame in our hearts shall shed new light and warmth on all that was purposed and willed in the Goetheanum, on all that we are now resolved to carry forward on the advancing wave of human evolution.

Let us then, my dear friends, recall at this time and write deeper in our hearts the words that I was able to speak to you over there in the Goetheanum almost in the very same moment of time a year ago. On that night I spoke somewhat in the following words : We are at the eve of a New Year, we must go forward to meet an oncoming Cosmic New Year. If the Goetheanum were still standing, this demand and this call could in this moment be renewed. It is no longer standing. The same call can, however, be uttered again on this New Year's Eve, can be uttered, as I believe, with redoubled power just because the Goetheanum is no longer there. Let us carry over the soul of the Goetheanum into the Cosmic New Year, let us try to erect in the new Goetheanum a worthy memorial to the old !

May our hearts be thus knit to the old Goetheanum, which we had perforce to give over to the elements. And may our hearts be closely knit to the spirit and the soul of this Goetheanum. And with this solemn pledge to the highest and the best that is in us, we will carry our life over not only into the New Year, but into the Cosmic New Year, we will go forward into it, strong for action, upheld and guided in soul and spirit.

My dear friends, you received me by rising in memory of the old Goetheanum. Let us now rise in token that we pledge ourselves to continue working in the spirit of the Goetheanum with the best and highest forces that we have within us. So be it. Amen.

And we will hold to this our solemn pledge, we will be true to it as long as we are able, we will hold to it with our will,—for our will it is that unites these human souls of ours with the souls of the Gods. We will remain faithful to the spirit in which at a certain moment of our life we first sought the Spiritual Science of the Goetheanum.

And let us understand and know how to keep the promise we have made.

IX

AS WE ARE TOGETHER for the last time during this Christmas Meeting which should be a source of strength and of vital importance for the Anthroposophical Movement, you will allow me to give this lecture as a supplement to the many vistas opened for us by the series of lectures just finished, while also giving tentative indications concerning the future of anthroposophical strivings.

When we look at the world to-day—and it has been the same for years now—destructive elements on a colossal scale are everywhere in evidence. Forces that are actively at work enable us to have forebodings of the abysses into which Western civilisation will continue to steer. When we think of those individuals who are outwardly the spiritual leaders in various domains of life, we shall perceive that these men are in the throes of an ominous, universal sleep. They think, or at least most of them were still thinking only a short time ago, that until the nineteenth century mankind was childish and primitive in respect of understanding and conceptions of the world. Then modern science appeared in its many branches and now—so it is thought—there exists something that must through all eternity be cultivated as the truth.

The people who think this are really giving way to extreme arrogance, only they are not aware of it. On the other hand there sometimes arises, even in men to-day, a premonition that things are not, after all, as I have described.

Some little time ago it was still possible for me to give lectures in Germany organised by the Wolff Bureau. They attracted extraordinarily large audiences so that the existence of a desire for Anthroposophy became obvious to many people. Among the many nonsensical utterances of

141

opponents there was one voice which to be sure was not much cleverer than the others in respect of content but which nevertheless indicated a remarkable premonition. It consisted in a newspaper report of one of the lectures I had given in Berlin. The notice was to this effect: When one listens to something of this kind, one becomes attentive to the fact that something is going on not only on the Earth—I am quoting the notice approximately—but in the whole Cosmos something is happening which summons men to adopt a spirituality different from what existed previously. Now, the forces of the Cosmos—not only earthly impulses—demand something from men. A kind of revolution is taking place in the Cosmos, the result of which must be the striving for a new spirituality.

Such utterances were constantly to be heard and were very worthy of note. The fact of the matter is this: the impulse that must be working in what is now to go out from Dornach must—as I emphasised from every possible point of view during the Meeting itself—be an impulse originating in the spiritual world, not on the Earth. Our striving here is to develop the strength to follow impulses from the spiritual world. That is why, in the evening lectures during this Christmas Meeting, I spoke of manifold impulses at work in the course of historical evolution in order that hearts could be opened for the reception of the spiritual impulses which have yet to stream into the earthly world, which are not derived from that world itself. Everything for which the earthly world hitherto has rightly been the vehicle, proceeded from the spiritual world. And if we are to achieve anything fruitful for the earthly world, the impulses for it must be brought from the spiritual world.

This prompts the assertion that the impulses we ought rightly to take with us from the Meeting for our further activity must be connected with great responsibility.

Let us think for a short time of the responsibility laid upon us by that Meeting. Anyone with a sense of the reality of the spiritual world could encounter many personalities during recent decades, and observing them spiritually experience bitter feelings regarding the future destiny of humanity on Earth. One could encounter one's fellow men on the Earth in the way that is possible spiritually and observe these human beings during their sleep while they are in the spiritual world with Ego and astral body, having left their physical and etheric bodies. During recent decades, explorations connected with the destinies of Egos and astral bodies during the sleep of human beings have resulted in knowledge calling for great responsibility on the part of those who possess it. One often saw souls, who had left their physical and etheric bodies during sleep, approaching the Guardian of the Threshold.

In the course of evolution the Guardian of the Threshold has been brought to men's consciousness in very many different ways. Many a legend, many a saga—for it is in this form, not in the form of historical tradition that things of the greatest importance are preserved—many a legend tells of how, in earlier times, this or that personality met the Guardian of the Threshold and was instructed by him how to enter the spiritual world and return again into the physical world. Every legitimate entry into the spiritual world must include the possibility of being able at any and every minute to return into the physical world and to live there as a practical, thoughtful human being, not as a visionary or as an ecstatic mystic.

Fundamentally speaking, it was this that was demanded by the Guardian of the Threshold through all the ages of human endeavours to enter the spiritual world. But notably in the last third of the nineteenth century hardly any human beings who succeeded in approaching the Guardian of the Threshold in waking consciousness were to be seen. In our present time, when it is historically incumbent upon the whole of mankind to encounter the Guardian of the Threshold in some form, one finds how souls during sleep approach the Guardian of the Threshold as Egos and astral bodies, and the pictures that are revealed are full of significance. The stern Guardian of the Threshold has around him groups of human souls in the state of sleep, souls who in waking

143

consciousness lack the strength to approach this Guardian of the Threshold. They approach him while they sleep.

When one watches the scene presented there, a thought connected with what I have called the seed of great and essential responsibility comes to one. The souls approaching the Guardian of the Threshold during the state of sleep plead with the consciousness then prevailing—in the waking state everything remains unconscious or subconscious—plead to be admitted into the spiritual world, to be allowed to cross the threshold. And in numberless cases one then hears the voice of the stern Guardian of the Threshold saying: For your own well-being you may not cross the threshold. You may not be allowed to enter the spiritual world. You must go back!—For if the Guardian of the Threshold were to permit such souls to enter the spiritual world, they would cross the threshold and enter that world with the concepts imparted to them by the schools, education and civilisation of to-day, with the concepts and ideas with which the human being is obliged to grow up from about the age of six to basically the end of his life on Earth.

The intrinsic character of these concepts and ideas is such that what a man has become through them in modern civilisation and education means that he enters the spiritual world paralysed in soul. Moreover, he would return to the physical world empty-headed in respect of thoughts and ideas. If the Guardian of the Threshold were not to reject many human souls of the modern age but allow them to enter the spiritual world, they would feel on awakening: I am incapable of thinking, my thoughts do not connect with my brain, I am obliged to go through the world void of thoughts. For such is the effect of the abstract ideas which man applies to everything to-day. With these ideas he can enter the spiritual world but not come forth from it again. And when one witnesses this scene which is experienced during sleep by more souls than is usually imagined, one feels: Oh! if only it were possible to protect these souls from having also to experience at death what they experience during sleep. For if the condition that is experienced in the presence of the

144

Guardian of the Threshold were to be repeated for a sufficient length of time, if civilisation were to remain long enough under the sway of what current education provides, then the souls of men would pass through the gates of death into the spiritual world but would be unable to bring any mental vigour into the next earthly life. With the thoughts prevailing to-day it is possible for a man to enter the spiritual world but he can only come out of it again paralysed in soul.

You see, modern civilisation adopts the form of spiritual life that has for so long been cultivated, but real life does not allow this. Civilisation as it now is might continue to progress for a time. During waking life souls would have no inkling of the existence of the Guardian of the Threshold and during sleep would be rejected by him in order to avoid mental paralysis; and this would finally result in a race of men being born in the future with no understanding, no possibility of applying ideas in their future earthly life; and all thinking, all ideation would vanish from the Earth. A diseased, purely instinctive human race would people the Earth. Evil feelings and unbridled emotions without the guiding power of ideas would take hold of the evolution of humanity. It is not only through observation of the souls confronting the Guardian of the Threshold—souls which can gain no entrance to the spiritual world—it is not only through observing this that a sorrowful picture is presented to the seer, but in a different connection there is another factor as well.

If on the journey of which I have spoken, when the souls of sleeping human beings confronting the Guardian of the Threshold can be observed, one is accompanied by a human being belonging not to Western but to Oriental civilisation, a terrible reproach of the whole of Western civilisation may be heard from him, to this effect: If things continue as they now are, when the human beings living to-day appear on Earth in new incarnations, the Earth will become barbaric. Human beings will live devoid of ideas, in instincts only. You Westerners have brought things to this pass because you have abandoned the ancient spirituality of the East.

A glimpse into the spiritual world such as I have described may well give rise to a sense of great responsibility. And here in Dornach there must be a place where for those human beings who have ears to hear, direct and significant experiences in the spiritual world can be described. Here there must be a place where sufficient strength is generated not merely to indicate in terms of the dialectic-empirical mentality of to-day that here or there little traces of spiritual reality exist. If Dornach is to fulfil its task, actual happenings in the spiritual world must be spoken of openly. Men must be able to hear of the impulses in the spiritual world which then pour into and control the natural world and Nature itself. In Dornach men must be able to hear of actual experiences, actual forces, actual Beings of the spiritual world. Here there must be the High School of true Spiritual Science. Henceforth we must not draw back when confronted by the shallowness of the scientific thoughts of to-day which, as I have described, lead in the state of sleep to the stern Guardian of the Threshold. In Dornach the strength must be acquired to confront and experience the spiritual world in its reality.

There must be no dialectical tirades from here on the subject of the inadequacy of modern scientific theory. I was obliged, however, to call attention to the position in which human beings are placed when confronting the Guardian of the Threshold on account of these scientific theories and their offshoots in the orthodox schools of to-day. If what has been said at this Christmas Meeting is sincerely applied in the life of soul, the Meeting will be a forceful impulse which the soul can then apply in the activity that is needed in this age so that in their next incarnations men may be able to confront the Guardian of the Threshold in the right way. This will ensure that civilisation in its own right can enable men to face and hold their own when confronting the Guardian of the Threshold.

Just compare the civilisation of to-day with that of earlier times during all of which men's thoughts and concepts were directed primarily to the supersensible world, to the Gods, to the world of productive, generative, creative forces. With concepts that were concerned primarily with the Gods, men were able to contemplate the earthly world and also to understand it in the light of these concepts and ideas. If with these concepts—worthy of the Gods as they were—a man came before the Guardian of the Threshold, the Guardian would say to him: You may pass, for you bring over the threshold into the supersensible world thoughts that were already directed to the supersensible world during your earthly life in a physical body. Thus when you return into the physical world of the senses you will have enough strength to protect you from being paralysed by the spectacle of the supersensible world.

To-day man develops concepts and ideas which in accordance with the genius of the age he wants to apply only to the material world. These concepts and ideas are concerned with every possible aspect of weight, measure and the like, but they have nothing to do with the Gods and are not worthy of the Gods. Hence to souls who have completely succumbed to materialistic ideas that are unworthy of the Gods, the voice of the Guardian of the Threshold thunders when they pass before him in the state of sleep: Do not cross the threshold! You have squandered your ideas on the world of the senses. Hence you must remain with them in the world of the senses. If you do not wish to be paralysed in your life of soul you may not enter the world of the Gods as long as you hold such ideas.

These things must be said, not in order to be the subject of argument but because every individual should let his mind and soul be permeated by them and thus develop the attitude of mind that should have been generated in him by this solemn Christmas Meeting of the Anthroposophical Society. For more important than anything else we take with us is the recognition of the spiritual world which gives the certainty that in Dornach there will be created a living centre of spiritual knowledge.

Hence a really splendid note was struck this morning when Dr. Zeylmans spoke in connection with the sphere of medicine, saying that it is no longer possible to-day for bridges to be built from orthodox science to what it is our aim to found in Dornach. If we were to speak of what it is hoped to develop in the sphere of medicine here by boasting that our products can stand the test of all modern clinical requirements, then we should never reach any definite goal. For then other people would simply say: That is just a new remedy; and we too have produced plenty of new remedies!

It is of essential importance that a branch of practical life such as medicine should be taken in the real sense into anthroposophical life. That is what I certainly understood to be Dr. Zeylmans' wish when he said this morning that an individual who becomes a doctor to-day really longs for something that gives impulses from a new corner of the world. In the domain of medicine this is just what will be done from here in the future, together with many another branch of genuine anthroposophical activity. It will be worked out now, with Dr. Wegman as my helper, as a system of medicine based upon Anthroposophy. It is a dire need of humanity and will soon be available. It is also my intention to establish as soon as possible a close relationship between the Goetheanum and the Clinic in Arlesheim that is proving to be so beneficial. The work there will be orientated entirely towards Anthroposophy. That is also Dr. Wegman's intention.

In speaking as he did, Dr. Zeylmans also indicated what attitude the Vorstand in Dornach will adopt in all spheres of anthroposophical activity. In future we shall know exactly how matters stand. We shall not say: let us bring Eurythmy to this or that town, for if people first see Eurythmy without hearing anything about Anthroposophy, Eurythmy will please them. Then, later on perhaps, they will come to us, and because they have liked Eurythmy and have heard that Anthroposophy is behind it, Anthroposophy too may please them! Or again, it may be said: In the practice of medicine people must be shown that ours are the right remedies and then they will buy them; later on they may discover that Anthroposophy is behind them and then they will come to Anthroposophy!

We must have the courage to realise that such procedure is dishonest and must be abandoned. Anthroposophy will then find its way in the world. Our striving for truth here in Dornach will in the future be without fanaticism, will be advocated honestly and candidly. Perhaps in this way we can make reparation for principles that have been gravely sinned against in recent years.

We must leave this Meeting, which has led to the Founding of the General Anthroposophical Society, not with trifling but with solemn thoughts. But I think that nobody need have experienced any pessimism as a result of what took place here at Christmas. We had, it is true, to pass the tragic ruins of the Goetheanum every day but I think that all those who climbed the hill and passed the ruins during the Meeting will have become aware of what our friends have understood in their hearts and that the following thought will have become a reality to them: Spiritual flames of fire will go forth from the new Goetheanum that will come into being in the future, for the blessing of mankind, will come into being through our activity and devotion. And the greater the courage with which to conduct the affairs of Anthroposophy that we take with us from this Meeting, the more effectively have we grasped the spiritual impulse of hope that has pervaded the Meeting.

The scene that I have described to you—the scene that is so often to be seen of modern man with the results of his civilisation and education facing the Guardian of the Threshold—this scene does not actually occur among perceptive Anthroposophists. But it does sometimes happen that this warning is necessary: You must develop the resolute courage to become aware of and avow your obedience to this voice from the spiritual world, for you have begun to wake. Courage will keep you wakeful; lack of courage—that and that alone could cause you to sleep.

The voice of exhortation to unfold courage and wakefulness—that is the other variant for Anthroposophists in the life of modern civilisation. Non-Anthroposophists hear the voice which says: Remain outside the spiritual world, for you have misused the ideas which are coined for purely earthly objects; you have amassed no ideas that are worthy of the Gods. Hence you would be paralysed on your return into the physical world of the senses. To the souls who are truly anthroposophical souls, however, it is said: You have now to be tested in respect only of your courage to avow adherence to the voice which because of the trend and inclination of your souls and hearts you can certainly hear and understand.

Yesterday, a year ago, we were watching the flames that were destroying the old Goetheanum, but just as we did not allow ourselves then to be interrupted in our continuation of the work, so to-day we are justified in hoping that when a physical Goetheanum will again be there, it will be merely the symbol of our spiritual Goetheanum which we will bear with us as idea when we now again go out into the world.

Over the Foundation Stone laid here will be erected the building in which the single stones will be the work achieved in every one of our Groups all over the world. We will now turn our thoughts to this work and become conscious of the responsibility of the men of to-day when they are standing before the Guardian of the Threshold who is obliged to forbid them entrance into the spiritual world.

Quite certainly it will never occur to us to feel anything except the deepest pain and sorrow for what happened to us a year ago. But of one thing we may be sure—everything in the world that has achieved some measure of greatness is born from pain. May our own pain be applied in such a way that a vigorous, light-filled Anthroposophical Society will come into being as the result of your work, my dear friends.

To this end we will ponder deeply on the words with which I began the Christmas Meeting and with which I want to end it. May it become for us a festival of consecration not only of a year's beginning but of the beginning of a turning-point of worlds, to which we will dedicate ourselves in selfless cultivation of the spiritual life:

Soul of Man!
Thou livest in the Limbs
Which bear thee through the world of Space
Into the ocean-being of the Spirit.
Practise *Spirit-Recollection*
In the depths of soul.
Where in the wielding
World-Creator-Life
Thine own   I
Comes to being
Within the   I   of God.
Then in the All-World-Being of Man
Thou wilt truly *live*.

For the Father-Spirit of the Heights holds sway
In Depths of Worlds begetting Life.
Spirits of Strength!
Let this ring out from the Heights
And in the Depths be echoed,
Speaking:
From God, Mankind has Being.
The Spirits hear it in East and West and North and South:
May human beings hear it!

Soul of Man!
Thou livest in the beat of Heart and Lung
Which leads thee through the rhythmic tides of Time
Into the feeling of thine own Soul-being.
Practise *Spirit-Mindfulness*
In balance of the soul,
Where the surging
Deeds of the World's Becoming
Do thine own   I
Unite
Unto the   I   of the World.
Then 'mid the weaving of the Soul of Man
Thou wilt truly *feel*.

For the Christ-Will in the encircling Round holds sway
In the Rhythms of the Worlds, blessing the Soul.
Spirits of Light!
Let this be fired from the East
And through the West be formed,
Speaking:
In Christ, Death becomes Life.
The Spirits hear it in East and West and North and South:
May human beings hear it!

Soul of Man!
Thou livest in the resting Head
Which from the ground of the Eternal
Opens to thee the Thoughts of Worlds.
Practise *Spirit-Vision*
In quietness of thought,
Where the eternal aims of Gods
World-Being's Light
On thine own   I
Bestow
For thy free Willing.
Then from the ground of the Spirit in Man
Thou wilt truly *think*.

For the Spirit's Universal Thoughts hold sway
In the Beings of all Worlds, craving for Light.
Spirits of Soul!
Let this be prayed in the Depths
And from the Heights be answered,
Speaking:
In the Spirit's Universal Thoughts, the Soul awakens.
The Spirits hear it in East and West and North and South:
May human beings hear it!

At the turning-point of Time
The Spirit-Light of the World
Entered the stream of Earthly Being.
Darkness of Night
Had held its sway;
Day-radiant Light
Poured into the souls of men;
Light that gives Warmth
To simple Shepherds' Hearts,
Light that enlightens
The wise Heads of Kings.

O Light Divine,
O Sun of Christ!
Warm Thou
Our Hearts
Enlighten Thou
Our Heads,
That good may become
What from our Hearts we would found
And from our Heads direct
With single purpose.

And so, my dear friends, carry out into the world your warm
hearts in which you have laid the Foundation Stone for the
Anthroposophical Society, carry out into the world these
warm hearts which promote strong, health-giving activity
in the world.   And help will be vouchsafed to you, enlighten-
ing your heads in what you would fain direct with single
purpose. We will set about this with all possible strength.

And if we prove to be worthy of this aim we shall see that a good star will hold sway over what is willed from here. Follow this good star, my dear friends! We shall see whither the Gods will lead us by the light of this star.

> O Light Divine,
> O Sun of Christ!
> Warm Thou
> Our Hearts
> Enlighten Thou
> Our Heads.

NOTES

p. 7   *our Christmas Gathering:* See *Die Weihnachtstagung zur Begründung der Allgemeinen Anthroposophischen Gesellschaft. Jahresausklang und Jahreswende 1923/24* by Rudolf Steiner, Collected Works, Dornach 1962.

p. 37   *a course of lectures:* See *Occult History. Historical Personalities and Events in the Light of Spiritual Science* by Rudolf Steiner, Anthroposophical Publishing Company, London, 1957.

p. 40   *that historic document:* The Epic of Gilgamesh was discovered in the ruins of a palace of Assurbanipal written in cuneiform characters on twelve tablets. This text is based on older Sumerian documents of which fragments remain.
Erech: Called Erech in the Bible (1 Moses 10, 10), the city is named Uruk in the cuneiform text.

p. 41   *Eabani:* The cuneiform text has Enkidu or Engidu.

p. 46   *Xisuthros:* This is the Sumerian name Ziusudra used by Berossus, priest of Bel in Babylon, who wrote a history of Babylon and Chaldea in Greek around 280 B.C. based on the archives of the Temple in Babylon. In cuneiform script it is Utnapishtim.

p. 49   *Mystery centre of Ephesus:* Rudolf Steiner spoke in detail about this place in the 6th lecture of *Mystery Knowledge and Mystery Centres*, Rudolf Steiner Press, London, 1973.

p. 50   *primeval conditions of the Earth:* See the 5th lecture in *Mystery Knowledge and Mystery Centres*.

p. 52   *Heraclitus:* Heraclitus of Ephesus, Greek philosopher. He lived around 500 B.C. and deposited his chief work in the Temple of Artemis. See *Christianity as*

Mystical Fact and the Mysteries of Antiquity by Rudolf Steiner, Rudolf Steiner Press, London, 1972.

p. 53   *Aristotle:* Greek philosopher from Stagira (384–322 B.C.). See *The Riddles of Philosophy* by Rudolf Steiner, Anthroposophic Press, New York, 1973.

        Alexander the Great: (356–323 B.C.). From 336 King of Macedonia. Died in Babylon.

p. 56   *Hibernian Mysteries:* See the 8th and 9th lectures in *Mystery Knowledge and Mystery Centres.*

p. 65   *The Song of Alexander:* Composed about 1125 by the Franconian priest Lamprecht; the first German secular epic poem.

p. 85   *Herodotus:* Herodotus of Halicarnassos, the first Greek historian, lived in the fifth century B.C. Wrote history of the Persian Wars.

p. 88   *the tyranny of Rome:* Justinian, Byzantine Emperor from 527–565, son of a peasant, sent an edict to Athens in 529 forbidding the teaching of philosophy and law. Thereupon the last seven Athenian philosophers left the Roman Empire and emigrated to Persia.

p. 93   *Julian the Apostate:* Flavius Claudius Julianus, called the Apostate by the Christians, was Roman Emperor from 361–363.

p. 99   *in recent lectures:* See note to page 56.

p. 103 *Jacob Boehme:* (1575–1624), mystic. See *Eleven European Mystics* by Rudolf Steiner, Rudolf Steiner Publications, New York, 1971.

        Paracelsus: Theophrastus Paracelsus (1493–1541), physician. See *Eleven European Mystics.*

        Valentine Weigel: (1533–1588), mystic. See *Eleven European Mystics.*

        Basil Valentine: Alchemist and Benedictine monk, lived from 1413 onwards in the Monastery of St. Peter in Erfurt. His writings were not discovered or printed till the beginning of the seventeenth century. See *Eleven European Mystics.*

pp. 104 and 105 *gymnast, rhetorician, professor:* Rudolf Steiner spoke in detail about this for instance in *A Modern Art of Education* by Rudolf Steiner, Rudolf Steiner Press, London, 1972 and *Human Values in Education* by Rudolf Steiner, Rudolf Steiner Press, London, 1971.

Some related books

by Rudolf Steiner
From Symptom to Reality in Modern History
Karmic Relationships—Esoteric Studies, Vols. I to VIII
The Life, Nature and Cultivation of Anthroposophy
The Foundation Stone

by other Authors
The Foundation Stone, A Commentary *by F. W. Zeylmans van Emmichoven*
Man and World in the Light of Anthroposophy *by S. C. Easton*

Some basic books by Rudolf Steiner
Occult Science—An Outline
Knowledge of the Higher Worlds—How is it achieved?
The Philosophy of Freedom
Theosophy
Christianity as Mystical Fact
Manifestations of Karma